WITHDRAWN
Damaged, Obsolete, or Surplus

Jackson County Library Services

DATE DUE   AUG 0 2

9/13/02			
OCT 22 '02			
29 0			
APR 1 4 200			
OCT 4 '03			
DEC 3 1 2003			
2-17 05			
4-18-05			
DEC 2 8 2005			
DEC 2 8 2005			
APR 4 '06			
MAY 03			
OCT 02 '06			
GAYLORD		PRINTED IN U.S.A.	

D1616334

Japanese COUNTRY STYLE

PUTTING NEW LIFE INTO OLD HOUSES

民 家 移 築　合掌造りに暮らす

YOSHIHIRO TAKISHITA
瀧下嘉弘

FOREWORD BY Peter M. Grilli

序：ピーター・M・グリリ／甘糟幸子

KODANSHA INTERNATIONAL

Tokyo · New York · London

JACKSON COUNTY LIBRARY SERVICES
MEDFORD, OREGON 97501

FOR

John, Katoji,
and
Kazu

ENGLISH TRANSLATION BY
Philip Harper and Juliet Winters Carpenter

JAPANESE TRANSLATION OF FOREWORD BY
Ayako Adachi

ALL LINE DRAWINGS (EXCEPT THOSE ON PAGES 24, 25, 66 & 124) BY
Tadamitsu Omori

EDITORIAL AND TECHNICAL ASSISTANCE BY
Azby Brown

NOTE: Some of the English text in this bilingual edition has been adapted to better serve the needs of the English-language readership.

Published by Kodansha International Ltd., 17–14 Otowa 1-chome, Bunkyo-ku, Tokyo 112-8652, and Kodansha America, Inc.

Distributed in the United States by Kodansha America, Inc., 575 Lexington Avenue, New York, New York 10022, and in the United Kingdom and continental Europe by Kodansha Europe Ltd., 95 Aldwych, London WC2B 4JF.

Copyright © 2002 by Yoshihiro Takishita. All rights reserved. Printed in Japan.

First edition, 2002

1 2 3 4 5 6 7 8 9   06 05 04 03 02
ISBN 4–7700–2761–3

www.thejapanpage.com

CONTENTS 目次

FOREWORD

Over the last three decades or so, casual visitors to Kamakura (and longtime residents as well) have wondered about a large, steeply sloped roof that seems to "grow" out of the top of Genjiyama, one of Kamakura's highest hills. Walking through the ancient town's leafy residential lanes or hiking along one of the many trails leading up into the hills, one's eyes are drawn, as if by a magnet, toward the powerful sculptural form of that roof that seems to crown the hilltop and the town itself. When I lived in Kamakura during the early 1970s, I was amused by the rumors circulating down in the town about the structure on the peak of Genjiyama and the identity of its inhabitants: some claimed it was the mountain villa of a former prime minister; no, said others, it was the sanctuary of a religious sect or a cult that worshipped the gods of the sea stretching out far below it. Once, with un-impeachable authority, I was informed by the proprietor of a little restaurant near Kamakura Station that the hilltop was actually the temporary asylum of a foreign ruler, living in exile in Japan but planning a revolution that would restore him to power in his homeland. This theory gained in credibility as local residents observed occasional motorcades of black limousines accom-panied by motorcycle police traveling up the steep hill toward the mysterious building at its peak.

I listened to these rumors with keen interest, but said noth-ing, of course, because I knew that the magnificent roof, which was all that was visible from the valley below, actually sheltered the home of my friends Yoshihiro and Reiko Takishita and Yoshi's adoptive American father, the journalist John Roderick. To me, there was no mystery about the place because I had visited it often and had frequently enjoyed the wonderful hospitality of the Takishitas. Still, I enjoyed participating in the mystery sur-rounding one of Kamakura's best-kept secrets because the *real* story of the mountaintop house, though lacking in sinister intrigue, is far more interesting and compelling than anything the rumor-mongers could cook.

I am delighted that Yoshi Takishita has finally told the story of his own house as well as the history and traditions that produced it. In this book he also tells the stories of a number of similar homes that he has created for friends and clients in Japan and abroad. With or without mysterious overtones, his own house

atop Genjiyama is, quite simply, one of the most magnificent abodes I have ever visited. Its power stems in part, of course, from its lofty location and the extraordinary vista of hills and ocean that it commands. But even more impressive is the build-ing itself, the all-embracing unity of its architectural components, and the obvious affection that has been lavished on it by its pre-sent owners. The house that now commands the most exalted hilltop in Kamakura traveled there from much humbler origins far away, and this book recounts that journey—a story that offers compelling messages about preservation and craft, about man's place in his natural surroundings, and about an aesthetic that transforms shelter into art.

Yoshihiro Takishita is a visionary who saw, with an eye untu-tored at first by architectural sciences, that the proud but crum-bling old farmhouses of his childhood in the remote mountains of Gifu could be transformed into great homes that satisfied the needs for comfort and convenience of twentieth- and twenty-first-century dwellers. Where others saw only hazard, discom-fort, and inconvenience in ancient structures built of heavy wooden beams and straw thatch, Takishita saw enduring beauty and strength. When others were ready to destroy the old farm-houses, trashing their proud traditions and exchanging them for the illusory convenience of prefabricated steel and plastic, Taki-shita stepped forward to rescue them, to preserve their majestic authority, and, by dismantling and reconstructing them, to trans-form them (in countless unseen ways) into warm, comfortable, and astonishingly beautiful homes.

Takishita's mission is fully in accord with the principles of the modern *mingei*, or "folk-craft," movement that has reintroduced to contemporary Japan the simple beauties of its agrarian past. His farmhouse-homes were originally crafted by hand, by carpen-ters and farmers whose hard work was motivated not by ego or enrichment but rather by function and necessity. Takishita's dwellings were restored by the same hands, guided by a similar spirit of dedication, and he has furnished them with a superb array of antique objects—ceramics, paintings, lacquerware, and metal crafts—all made with comparable craftsmanship and zeal. That spirit was perhaps best expressed by the ideals of Yanagi Soetsu, the philosopher and aesthetician who attributed the

"The house on the hill."　　丘の上に甦った合掌造り。

enduring beauty of ancient crafts to "the hand of the Buddha": "If there is beauty here, it does not stem from the power of a single individual but must be seen as the work of a power surpassing the people involved, operating behind the scenes to endow the object with beauty. To put the matter simply, the other power, the hand of the Buddha, is at work in the beauty of the anonymous object."

This book recounts Yoshihiro Takishita's discovery of the ageless beauty of craft in Japan's rural traditions and his remarkable dedication to giving modern meaning to ancient architectural truths. The "story" of the book is the process of rebuilding and restoring his own home and fifteen other old Japanese farmhouses. But there is much more here than an account of foundation-posts

and roof-beams and joinery. Takishita's personal story is a journey of self-discovery with deep significance for modern Japan's confrontation with its own past. His vision, craftsmanship, and dedication have brought these farmhouses back to life, giving them a new identity and new meaning. There can be no question that guiding his handiwork and inspiring his efforts has been something more—perhaps, indeed, "the hand of the Buddha."

PETER M. GRILLI
President, Japan Society of Boston

序文

鎌倉へふらりとやってくる観光客や長くその地に住む人たちは、過去30年以上もの間、鎌倉で一番高い丘の一つ源氏山の頂上に見える、大きく切り立った屋根を不思議に思っていた。緑に包まれた古都の路地を歩いていたり、丘に通じる小道を散策していたりすると、その屋根の力強い彫刻的な造形に、磁石のように目が吸い寄せられるのだ。それはまるで丘の上に載せられた冠のように見えた。私が鎌倉に住んでいた1970年代の初めころ、源氏山の建物とその居住者の正体について、街にはおもしろい噂が広まっていた。元首相の山荘なのだという人もいれば、いや、遠く眼下に広がる海の神をあがめる宗教団体の聖地なのだという人もいた。あるとき私は、鎌倉駅近くの小さなレストランのオーナーから、確実な情報としてこんな話を聞いた。丘の上の家は、じつはある外国の指導者の隠れ家であり、日本に亡命してきたが再び祖国で権力を握るため革命を計画しているのだという。ときおり白バイを伴った黒いリムジンの列が、頂上のミステリアスな建物めざして険しい丘を登っていくのが目撃されたことから、これは信憑性のある説となった。

私はこれらの噂を非常に興味ぶかく聞いていたが、もちろん自分からは何もいわなかった。なぜなら、街からは素晴らしい屋根しか見えなかったが、その屋根の下には、私の友人の瀧下嘉弘と瀧下怜子、そして彼のアメリカ人の養父でジャーナリストのジョン・ローデリックが住んでいるということを知っていたからである。私はそこをしばしば訪ねていたし、よく瀧下家の素晴らしいもてなしにあずかっていたのだ。それでも、鎌倉でもっともかたく守られている秘密をめぐるミステリーに参加して楽しんでいた。この丘の上の家の本当の姿は、邪悪な陰謀に欠けてはいたけれど、ウワサに夢中になっている人たちが作り上げる話より、はるかにおもしろく心引かれるものだった。

瀧下嘉弘がついに自分自身の家のこと、それを生み出した歴史や伝統について語ってくれたとはうれしいことだ。本書で彼は友人や顧客のために作った数々の家について語っている。ミステリアスな意味合いがあろうとなかろうと、源氏山の頂上にある彼の家は、まさに私が訪れたなかでもっとも素晴らしい住まいの一つだ。その力強さは、もちろんそびえたつ山の上であるということと、丘からの類いまれな眺望、眼下に見おろす海などから来るものでもあるが、より印象的なのは建物そのものである。それぞれの建築要素が一体となって、まるで抱かれているような統一感があり、現在の主人からたっぷりと注がれている愛情が感じられるのだ。鎌倉でもっとも注目されているこの家は、はるか遠く、ずっと控えめな土地からここにやってきた。本書はその旅をたどり、保存と技術、本来の環境の中での人の

あり方、そして住まいを芸術に変える美学について、説得力あふれるメッセージを伝えるものなのである。

瀧下嘉弘は、建築学の教育に最初から染まることのなかった夢想家である。岐阜の辺鄙な山の中にある立派な、しかし崩れそうな古い農家を見て、彼はこれを20世紀、21世紀の居住者たちが望む快適さや便利さをもった素晴らしい家に変えられると考えた。他の人が見れば、重い木の梁とわらの屋根でできた、危険で不快で不便な、ただの大昔の建物だが、瀧下はそこに永遠の美と力強さを見たのである。古い農家を壊し、誇るべき伝統を打ち砕き、規格品の鋼やプラスチックの便利さという幻想と交換しようとしている人たちがいる一方で、瀧下は果敢にもそれらを救い、堂々とした威厳を保存し、解体と再建によって(目には見えない数えきれないほどの方法によって)、温かく快適で美しい家々に変えたのである。

瀧下の使命は、かつての農村生活の簡潔な美を再評価する現代の民芸運動と完全に一致している。彼の手がける移築民家は、もともと大工や農民の手で建てられたもので、そういった人々は自負心や見た目の華やかさのためでなく、むしろ実用本位の機能と必要性をめざして懸命に働いていたのである。瀧下の家はそれと同じ手によって、同様の献身的な姿勢で再建された。そして彼はこの家にみごとな骨董品を並べた。陶器、絵画、漆器、金属工芸――どれも家を建てたときと同様の職人技と熱意によって作られたものだ。その精神は、おそらく柳宗悦の掲げた理想にもっともよく表現されているだろう。柳は哲学者にして美学者であり、過去の工芸の永遠の美を「釈迦の手によるもの」とした。そこに美があるとき、それは一人の個人の力から生まれるものではなく、作品に美を与えるために舞台裏で関与し、作業している人々を超えた力の作用として見られるに違いない。簡単にいうと、他力、すなわち「釈迦の手」が匿名の作品の美に作用しているのである。

本書は、日本の農村に生き続けてきた永遠の美の発見と、伝統的な建築の真理に現代的な意味を与えた彼の並外れた献身ぶりを語っている。内容は、瀧下邸とその他15軒の古い日本の農家の再建と修復の過程をつづったものである。しかしここには、支柱や屋根の梁、木組みなどの説明以上のものがある。彼の先見性と職人的な技、そして献身的態度は、これらの農家を甦らせ新しい個性と新しい意味合いを与えた。彼の仕事を導きその努力を鼓舞したのは、何かより大きなものであることに間違いはない――それはおそらく、まさに「釈迦の手」なのである。

ピーター・M・グリリ
ジャパン・ソサエティ(ボストン)理事長

THE APPEAL OF *MINKA*

Among all the houses that Mr. Takishita has moved and reconstructed, the old-fashioned *gassho zukuri*-style farmhouse that was his fifth project is now our home. Though small as such houses go, it makes us feel that we are inhabiting a different era. The structure is solid, with a high ceiling supported by wide columns and beams. Beyond the spaciousness of the design, we take pleasure in thinking back on the huge trees that spent years growing on mountainsides; the villagers turning out en masse to cut and trim them; the old techniques used to craft the house in traditional *gassho* style, with sloping gabled roofs; and the generations of families who lived here before us, our lives linked now in a continuum with theirs.

The impetus for our acquisition of the house came from dramatist Kuniko Mukoda. "There's an interesting young antique dealer up in the mountains," she told us, inspiring us one day to set out nonchalantly for a look at the Takishita House. Passing from the dimly lit *doma*, or earthen-floored entryway, into the living area, we saw overhead a ceiling as high and spacious as that of a temple. The massive scale of the beams—no hint of which showed from the outside—was surprising and at the same time vaguely nostalgic. Rather than looking at old bowls and plates as planned, we ended up eagerly exploring the Takishita House, as well as the Roderick House next door.

"Are there any smaller *minka*?" asked my husband, who had been planning to renovate our own decrepit house. Over the protestations of Mukoda, who thought those beams would be "oppressive as hell" to live with, we pushed ahead, and soon heard from Takishita that he had found just the thing. I traipsed through falling snow to watch the house being dismantled in the distant village of Ono, Fukui Prefecture. By the end of spring, reconstruction was underway, and a year later the house was finished. The space under its broad beams radiates peace and comfort. Friends who come by at first all said the same thing: "It's so relaxing here, I never want to leave!" They did seem to linger more than before, in fact.

I cannot forget a story I heard from Mr. Takishita's wife, Reiko. Soon after they were married, the young couple went to see an old abandoned farmhouse on the upper reaches of the Kuzuryu River in Ono. No sooner did they step inside the door than he burst out, eyes shining, "Isn't that beautiful!" The place he indicated was covered with thick rolls of dust and cobwebs. Reiko confesses that in that moment, she worried about her new husband's sanity. I must admit that when I went to Ono that winter to watch that tumbledown old farmhouse being taken apart, I wondered anxiously whether the effort and expense of moving and rebuilding it could possibly be justified.

It takes a special gift to see the true value of what appears as junk to the ordinary eye. Mr. Takishita has an instinctive ability to see through layers of dirt and rubbish—the accumulated grime of years of daily living—down to the essential beauty of the underlying form, and the sturdiness of a building's structure.

Above all, the structure is solid, permitting all manner of free experimentation. The charm of the reconstructed house probably has a lot to do with the fact that Mr. Takishita never studied architecture in university and approaches design strictly from the perspective of a home's future inhabitants and what will make them happy. Above the beams in the Takishita living room, in the space formed by the steep angle of the joined roofs, is a free arrangement of endless little rooms—each with its ladder and stairway—that conveys the joy of children playing at hide-and-seek.

The young man I recall from those early days has now overseen the rebuilding of thirty *gassho zukuri* farmhouses, thus saving them from demolishment. Now well into his fifties, he exudes confidence and calm. Apparently Mr. Takishita wishes to rest awhile from the work he has done so well for so long, and consider his next step. I look forward with pleasure to his next bold leap. I have often wished for a bird's-eye view of Takishita's s architecture, a wish that this book will go far to answer.

SACHIKO AMAKASU

瀧下建築の魅力

　瀧下さんの手がけた移築のなかで、五番目に建てた合掌造りが私たちの住まいだ。特別に小さな家なのだが、ここに住む前とそれからでは別の時間のなかにいるような気がする。太い柱と梁に支えられた天井は高く、たしかにどっしりとした建物だ。だが、空間の大きさだけでなく、この木々が山の中で育った年月、村中総出で伐りだし、伝統通りの工法で合掌の家を建て、そこで営まれてきた何世代にもわたる暮らし、その暮らしに連なっている、という感覚は不思議に心の落ち着くものだった。

　きっかけは向田邦子さんだった。「山の上に面白い骨董青年がいるそうよ」と誘われて何気なく瀧下邸にでかけた。薄暗い土間を通って居間に一歩踏み入れると、頭上に伽藍のような空間が広がっていた。外観からは想像もできなかった迫力のある梁の大きさに驚き、同時に不思議な懐かしさも感じた。私たちは当初の目的だった古い壺や皿鉢の見学よりも、瀧下邸と、並んで建っていたロドリック邸の探検に熱中してしまった。

　「もう少し小ぶりな民家はありませんか」と夫が聞いたのは、老朽化したわが家の半分を改築する予定があったからだった。「よしなさい。あんな太い梁の下で毎日暮らすのはうっとおしい」という向田さんの忠告をよそに、意外な速さで瀧下青年から恰好の家があった、と連絡が入った。私は雪の降る福井県の大野村へ解体現場を見に行き、春の終わりには工事が始まった。一年の後完成してみると、太い梁の下はのびやかで心地良い空間だった。友人たちが遊びきては「ここは落ち着くね。つい長居してしまう」と同じような口調でいい、たしかに帰りの時間はどの人も遅くなった。

　忘れられない話を夫人の怜子さんから聞いた。結婚して間もないころ、九頭竜川の上流に廃屋となった農家を見にいった時のこと、荒れ果てた家に入るなり、瀧下さんが「美しいでしょう」と目を輝かせていう。指さしたところにはクモの巣が張り、土ぼこりがたまっている。怜子さんは結婚したばかりの夫を「頭がおかしいんじゃないか」といぶかったそうだ。じつは私も大野村へ解体工事を見にいった時、生活の猥雑さの残る、うらぶれた小さな家を見て、移築する価値があるのか、と不安になったものだった。

　凡人の眼にはただの廃屋にしか見えないものの中に見るべきものを見るのが才能ではないだろうか。瀧下さんは塵芥（ちり・あくた）、生活の垢に覆われたものの下から、合掌造りのもつ基本の美しさ、なによりもその構造のたしかさを感知する本能をもった人なのだ。

　まず、ゆるぎのない構造がある。だから自由な発想の数々が生きてくる。もしかしたら大学では建築を専攻せずに、住む者の楽しさから建築デザインを考えたことも幸いしたのかもしれない。瀧下邸の広間の梁の上、合掌の屋根にかかえられた空間にある、小さな梯子や階段と、いくつもの小部屋との組み合わせの自在さはかくれんぼする子供の楽しさだ。

　あの時青年だった瀧下さんは、消えていく合掌造りの移築を三十棟もみごとに移築させ、今では自信と落ち着きをもつ五十代となった。聞けば、しばらくは移築の仕事を休んで次の展望を得たいそうだ。新しい飛躍を期待している。いつかは瀧下建築を俯瞰するように眺めてみたい、と願っていたが、この一冊が願いの半分はかなえてくれることだろう。

甘糟幸子

A cozy study in a second-story loft.　　　屋根裏に作られた小さな書斎。

chapter 1

ENCOUNTERING THE JAPANESE FOLK HOUSE

I was born and raised in a town called Shirotori, in the Gujo region of Gifu Prefecture. It is situated northwest of the town of Gujo Hachiman (famous for its Bon Festival), in amongst the mountains of the higher reaches of the Nagara River. About thirty kilometers (nineteen miles) north of Shirotori, along the Gujo Highway, is a village called Shokawa. When I was a junior high school student, I heard that the Miboro Dam would be constructed there and went to see the site. At that time, I saw my first *gassho zukuri* house, a type of traditional folk dwelling (*minka*) with a steep roof in the shape of "praying hands" (*gassho*). It made a powerful—even a shocking—impression on me. It was the house of the Toyama family and one of the largest examples of the type. Currently, this house receives many visitors, having become a museum, but, at that time, old dwellings such as this were being pulled down one after another to make way for the construction of the dam. Some houses had fortunately escaped being pulled down by being moved to the city, and this was the first time I ever heard the term *minka ichiku*: the removal and reconstruction of *minka* dwellings. Since then, the expression has come to dominate my life.

In 1963, after entering a university in Tokyo, I had an experience that was to play a decisive role in my way of life from then on. At an acquaintance's suggestion, I went to look at a late Edo-period (1600–1868) dwelling, originally from Chichibu, in Saitama. I later learned that this house, which had been moved and reassembled in Tokyo's Roppongi district, was known as Senri-an and belonged to Meredith Weatherby, the American chairman of a publishing firm that introduces Japanese art overseas.

I was captivated by the massive, lustrous central pillar, the high ceiling, and the curved black beams that snaked beneath it, not to mention the breathtakingly impressive living room, as seen from the mezzanine floor. A collection of Japanese antiques decorated the room, making the expanse of this old dwelling yet more appealing. Wooden sculptures of the gods of wind and thunder that were perched on the beams in the living room are still as clear in my mind's eye as if I had seen them yesterday.

At that time, I lived with my foster father, John Roderick, in a rented house halfway up Mount Nagoe in Kamakura. With a wide view of the sea, it was a perfect location, though a temporary accommodation. After seeing the Weatherby House, our longing for the house of our dreams, a restored *minka*, became ever

stronger. Then, one day, in the year after the 1964 Tokyo Olympics, we had welcome news from my mother, who ran a kimono shop in my hometown of Shirotori. She told me that part of a village called Izumi, about three hours by car to the west, was due to be submerged by the construction of a dam, and that we could obtain one of the *minka*. The fact that the Naka Ise district, which is where Izumi is situated, was also the site of an *ochiudo* legend (of the flight of the defeated Heike soldiers in the twelfth century) enhanced its appeal.

I lost no time in having my parents show my foster father and me to the village. The condition of the narrow road was not good, and it seemed like it would wind on deep between the mountains forever. When we finally arrived at Naka Ise, we found a small hamlet of about a dozen dwellings, all in the *gassho zukuri* style with thatched roofs. I had the impression that I had stumbled back into the Edo period.

It must have been just after the end of the rice harvest, when the villagers were catching their breath, and they regarded our party with curious looks. I still cannot forget the moment I set foot in the house of the village headman, as the assembled villagers stared. We stepped up from the earthen floor into the house itself, and, as my eyes became accustomed to the semi-darkness inside, I could make out the curved beams, which looked as if they were flying beneath the ceiling. "This is it!" I thought, moved almost to the point of agitation. At the same moment, I noticed an odor, which seemed somehow very comforting. Was this the smell engendered by long years of living at one with nature? Time seemed to flow comfortably in this space that enveloped me so peacefully. "This is the only house I could ever want," I thought. To our astonishment, the owner, a descendant of the Heike, offered it to us as a gift.

Although we had obtained the house itself, it was to be a long time before we could finally live in it. First, we had to look for land. After a year and a half of searching here and there, we eventually found a suitable location on Kamakura's Genjiyama mountain, overlooking Mount Fuji and Sagami Bay, and the moment of actually transferring the dwelling came at last. Carpenters from Gujo, heir to the master's tradition of the Hida region of Gifu, began the work, and I also helped with the transfer as much as possible. It was more interesting and fulfilling than I had expected.

私が生まれ育った所は、岐阜県郡上郡の白鳥町という。盆踊りで有名な郡上八幡の西北、長良川上流の山間いの町である。この白鳥町から郡上街道を60kmほど北上した所に白川村がある。私が中学生の時、そこにダム（御母衣ダム）が建設されると聞いて見学に行ったことがある。私はこの時初めて合掌造りの民家というものを見て、ほとんど衝撃的ともいえるほど強烈な印象を受けた。これが合掌造りでも最大級といわれる遠山家であった。この家は現在、記念館となって多くの見学者を集めているが、当時は多くの民家がダム建設のために次々と取り壊されていた。運良く取り壊しをまぬがれ都会に移築される家もあると聞き、これが「民家移築」という言葉との初めての出会いであった。以来、「移築」という言葉はずっと私を支配することになった。

1963年、東京の大学に入学した私は、それ以後の生き方に決定的な影響を与える貴重な体験をした。ある人の伝手で、東京の六本木に移築された江戸時代末期の秩父の民家を見たことだ。後にこの家は「千里庵」とよばれていることを知るが、持ち主はウェザビー氏といって日本美術を海外に紹介する出版社の会長であった。

太く光沢のある大黒柱、高い天井とその下を縫うように走る黒々として曲った梁、中二階の障子を開けて見おろすとハッと息をのむほど堂々としたリビングルーム。家の中には、日本の骨董コレクションが場所を得て置かれており、この古民家の空間を一層魅力的にしていた。居間の梁上に置かれた「風神雷神」の木彫は、今でも生き生きした映像として脳裏に焼きついている。

当時私は、養父ロデリックとともに鎌倉は名越にある山の中腹に借家住まいをしていた。海を一望する絶好のロケーションではあったが、仮住まいにはちがいない。自分たちの思いどおりの家が欲しいという思いはだんだん強くなっていた。そんなある日、たしか東京オリンピック（1964年）の翌年だったが、故郷で呉服商を営む母から耳よりな話を聞いた。私の実家のある白鳥町から車で西へ30kmほど行った所にある福井県の和泉村（穴馬郷）の一部が、ダム建設のため水没することになり、その地の庄屋だった民家が手に入る、というのである。この民家のある中伊勢という地域は平家の落人伝説もある所だった。

私は、さっそく養父とともに両親の案内でその村に行ってみたが、当時は道路事情も悪く、深い山中は細い道がくねくねとどこまでも続くかに思えた。土煙をあげながらようやく辿り着いた中伊勢は、民家12軒ほどの小さな集落で、すべて茅葺き屋根の合掌造りであった。私はあたかも江戸時代に迷い込んだような錯覚を覚えた。

村人たちは稲の刈り入れも終って一息ついていた時だったのだ

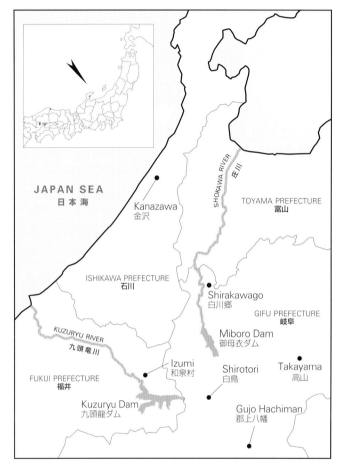

ろう。私たち一行を好奇の眼差しで眺めていた。彼らの視線に囲まれながらその庄屋だった家に足を踏み入れた瞬間を、私は今でも忘れることができない。土間から屋内に上がり内部の薄暗さに眼が慣れてくると、天井の下を飛んでいるかのような曲り木がまず目に入った。「これだ！」と私は心躍る感動を覚えた。同時にふっと心がなごむような「匂い」に気づいた。それは長い間、生活と自然が一体となって醸しだされてきた「匂い」なのか。私を包み込んでくれるやすらかな空間にゆったりと時間が流れる。私が欲しい家はこれ以外にないと思った。そしてすぐに私たちはご当主である、野村経利氏からこの家を譲り受けることにしたのである。

民家そのものは手に入ったものの、住まいとして実現するにはさらに長い月日を要した。まず土地を探さなければならない。あちらこちらを見て回った結果、富士山と相模湾を望む鎌倉の源氏山に格好の地を得るまでには一年半を費していた。

そしてようやく民家移築の開始である。「飛騨の匠」の伝統を受け継ぐ郡上の大工さんが動き出し、私もできるだけ移築の手伝いをしながら想像以上に面白く充実した日々を過ごした。

With the cooperation of a number of people, the house was finally completed, and I once again experienced the thrill I had as a boy upon seeing the Toyama family home for the first time and on seeing Senri-an in Roppongi. But delighted as I was to have realized my long-standing dream, I felt physically and mentally weary. I had graduated from university, and with no clear view of my future career, I set off overseas in search of a new beginning. It was a haphazard, spur-of-the-moment, shoestring journey around Europe, the Middle East, Africa, and the United States, but it brought me into contact with all kinds of different cultures and taught me the habit of observing and learning from things. In particular, my firsthand contact with the "stone-building" culture of the West had, almost without my knowing it, strengthened the attractions for me of Japan's "wooden buildings." In later life, on many occasions and in many places, I have had cause to think of this journey as an incomparably rich source of fertilization in my life.

About a year and a half after setting out, I started to feel the urge to return to Japan. Little by little, the fresh impressions I had initially gotten from traveling were disappearing. Mentally, I formed an image of a possible lifestyle after returning home. Barely waiting to unpack, I visited an old friend, and, on the basis of his advice and my enthusiasm for places like Senri-an, I decided to open an antique business in my home on Genjiyama, in Kamakura.

I decorated my two-story house, with its *gassho* frame, with folk craft objects and other antiques, using them in my everyday life, and selling them when there was a buyer. I saw customers by appointment only, a very congenial system. When I actually opened for business, I was fortunate in meeting many wonderful, discerning customers. Word of mouth helped too, and business went smoothly.

At one point, the Salomons, an American businessman and his Japanese wife, came looking for antiques. After a quick look around, the husband said to his wife, "Choose anything you like as a birthday present." She immediately replied, "What I want is a house like this!" As a result, I later came to build a vacation home for them in Karuizawa, but even then I never would have thought that this would become my life's work. However, after finishing the Salomon House, I found myself with more and more similar work, transferring and reassembling old houses. In retrospect, it was that single comment by Mrs. Salomon that prompted me to devote my life to the reconstruction of old houses.

After this, at the time when I contracted to build my fourth house, I had a peculiar experience. After purifying the four corners of the house with ritual salt and saké, I rubbed the central pillar over and over again, marveling at its long years of service and imagining its history. Once the thatch had been taken off, the whole primitive structure of the roof was revealed, lashed

大勢の人の協力で家が完成した時、私の胸には、少年時代に初めて見た遠山家や、先年目にした六本木の「千里庵」から受けた感動が再び甦ってきた。こうして、住まいへの年来の思いが実現したことを喜ぶ一方で、心身の疲労も重なり、また大学は卒業したものの、社会人としての将来の見通しもないまま、転機を求めて海外へ放浪の旅に出た。ヨーロッパ、中近東、アフリカから、アメリカへと無計画で気ままな貧乏旅行だったが、先々でさまざまな異文化に接し、ものを見る眼を養い、考える機会と習慣をもつことができた。なかでも、西欧の「石」の文化と身近に接することで、日本の「木」の文化のもつ魅力が、いつしか心の底にどっしりと腰を据えていた。この時の旅は私の人生に例えようもなく豊かな肥料を与えてくれたと、後々のいろいろな場面で思いあたっている。

旅に出て一年半、私はようやく日本に帰る気になった。旅から得る新鮮な感動が徐々に無くなっていくことに気づき始めたからである。私の頭には、帰国後の生き方に、あるイメージが湧いていた。旅の荷をほどくのももどかしく、私は旧知の先輩を訪ね、彼のアドバイスとかつて「千里庵」で感動した体験をヒントに、鎌倉の源氏山の自宅で骨董屋を開く決心をした。合掌組みの二階家を古民芸や骨董で飾り、日常自分でも使いながら買手があれば売る、しかもお客に対しては完全予約制という虫のよい商売方法だったが、実際に始めてみると、物を見極めるしっかりした眼識をもった素晴らしいお客との出会いに恵まれ、くちコミもあってか、仕事は順調であった。

あるとき、アメリカ人と日本人女性のご夫婦が骨董を求めに訪れた。ざっと見て回った後、ご主人は夫人に、「誕生日のプレゼントに、なんでも好きなものを選びなさい」といった。彼女は即座に、「私、こんな家が欲しいわ」と答えた。このことがきっかけで後に軽井沢に彼らサロモン夫妻の別荘を建てることになったのだが、その時は、よもやこれが私の終生の仕事になるなどとは思いもしなかった。しかしサロモン邸が竣工するころになると、次々に民家移築の仕事が舞い込むようになった。思えば、サロモン夫人の一言が民家移築を生涯の仕事とするきっかけになったといえるだろう。

その後、4軒目に請負った軽井沢の別荘を建てるために、福井県池田町で民家の解体をしていた時、私は奇妙としかいいようのない体験をした。家の四方を塩と酒で清めたあと、私は何度も大黒柱をさすりながら長年の労をねぎらい、この家の歴史に思いを馳せた。屋根の茅を取り払うと、合掌組みとモヤを縄で結んだ原始的な屋根の構造が現われる。次に合掌組みを地面におろすとその下には、あの曲り木の梁のみごとな組み合わせが頑丈な柱とともに

The Toyama House in the village of Shirakawa, Gifu Prefecture. An excellent example of the *gassho zukuri* ("praying hands") roof.

合掌造りの代表といわれる白川郷にある遠山家住宅。中学生の時この遠山家を見て感激した。

15

Once the thatch is removed, the structure emerges.
解体作業の始まり。古い茅をおろし終えると合掌屋根の下地材が現れる。

together from the *gassho* frame and brushwood. Next, the roof beams were lowered to the ground, and there emerged from beneath them the form of the wonderful interlocking beams of curved timber as well as the sturdy pillars. Once the straw mats and bamboo had been lowered from the roof space and the earthen walls had been removed from between the pillars, the bare skeleton of the house was revealed. These were the main beams and pillars. Bulky and robust and extremely beautiful, they appeared sculptural, with a lifelike dignity. It was so enchanting that I would happily have left it as it was to be able to gaze at it forever. The peculiar experience I mentioned came a few moments later, when the beams and pillars were finally dismantled and laid on the ground. The vital light they had radiated a moment ago was lost in an instant. What remained were a few worn old pieces of timber. The mortises and joints that had been cut here and there were painful to look at, like great wounds in the wood: it was a truly pathetic sight. Removed from their role of forming the frame of the house, the pillars and beams had simply become some old timber. In this cruel state the lumber seemed to be speaking to me. I seemed to hear voices imploring me to do something. The one task I could undertake in response to the wordless pleas for attention was, of course, to revive them through relocation and reconstruction. When the pillars and beams were reassembled as a contemporary home, when that space had been restored, *that* was when the beautiful luster would shine forth once more.

And so I became ever more entranced by the work of relocating and reconstructing old *minka*. The joy of seeing a house finished is different every time, and there is nothing better; it more than makes up for the two or three years of toil it takes to get the job done. Before I knew it, thirty houses had been transplanted and were thriving in their new locations.

姿を現わす。天井の筵や煤竹をおろし、柱と柱の間の壁土を落とすと民家の骨格だけが姿を現わした。家の基本的構造である軸組の柱と梁だ。その太くたくましい、それでいて優美な姿は品格のある生きた彫刻のように思われた。いつまでもこのままにしてずっと眺めていたいほど魅力的であった。奇妙な体験をしたのは、解体工事が進んだ柱や梁が地面に横たえられた瞬間である。つい先ほどまで柱や梁が放っていた生き生きとした光はあっという間に消え失せ、ただの媒けた古い材木と化していた。所々に空けられたホゾ穴や欠き込みはあたかも、大きな傷を負ったように痛々しく、哀れにさえ見えた。柱と梁は、家の骨格を形成する役目から解き放たれたとき、ただ単に古ぼけた材木になってしまったのである。この無残な姿の材木は私に何かを語りかけてくる。それは、何とかしてくれという哀願の声にも聞えた。その木の無言の叫びに応える作業こそ民家移築・再生ではないだろうか。柱や梁の骨格は現代の住宅として再生し、空間を取り戻した瞬間、再び生き生きとした輝きを放ってくれるのである。

　私はこうして古民家の移築再生という仕事に魅せられていった。完成したときの喜びは、個々の違いはあれ、何にも例えがたい。工期2～3年という長い間の苦労も忘れさせてくれるに余りあった。気がつけば30棟の古民家に新天地で生命を吹き込んでいたのである。

The main beams and posts of a *gassho zukuri minka*.
解体が進み柱と梁が全容を現す。

第2章 合掌造り民家の歴史と村の暮らし

chapter 2

THE HISTORY OF *GASSHO ZUKURI* DWELLINGS AND VILLAGE LIFE

Gassho zukuri dwellings are found primarily in central Gifu Prefecture and the mountainous regions of Toyama Prefecture, all areas of heavy snowfall. The Shokawa river, whose source is in central Gifu Prefecture, flows through the remote regions of the Miboro Dam, Shirakawago village, Gokayama district, and Shokawa village before flowing into Toyama Bay. *Gassho zukuri* villages are situated here and there along its banks. Of these, the groups of dwellings in Shirakawago and Gokayama in particular are famous tourist spots, and were registered by UNESCO as World Heritage Sites in 1995.

According to legend, after being defeated by Kiso Yoshinaka at the Battle of Kurikara Pass in 1183, the surviving Heike soldiers lived in secret in Shirakawago village. Isolated like an island far from shore, these remote mountain settlements are encircled to the east by the Hida Mountains, and to the west by Mount Hakusan. Since about ninety percent of the land is forested and mountainous, arable land is extremely scarce.

As it was blessed with a copious supply of high quality, very old timber, this region offered lumber as tribute to the shoguns during a portion of the Edo period (1600–1868). Japanese cedar, zelkova, pine, camphor, and chestnut wood were used in building the frames of *gassho zukuri* dwellings, and there was also high-grade Japanese cypress from old trees. These went as tax payments to the authorities, and were sold to other regions to raise revenue. The Hida region in contemporary Gifu Prefecture still has one of the most flourishing forestry districts of Japan today.

Besides its wealth of timber, another characteristic of the area is the large number of followers of the Jodo (Pure Land) sect of Buddhism, who have lived there for centuries. This is due to the influence of the priest Rennyo (1415–99), the eighth head abbot of the Honganji temple in Kyoto, who was known as "the savior of the Jodo sect" and who carried out vigorous missionary work in the mid Muromachi period (1338–1573) in the Hokuriku and Hida areas, using Echizen Yoshizaki as a base. The Jodo sect, founded by the monk Shinran, essentially believes that one should surrender one's individual will and trust entirely in Buddha. The followers in this district are not so-called funeral Buddhists, who practice their religion only at funerals, but true believers. Consequently, *gassho zukuri* dwellings generally have a separate altar room, and homes equipped with splendid altars (*butsudan*) are common even today.

In the writings of Yanagi Soetsu (1889–1961), known for the *mingei* (folk crafts) movement, we find the following on the subject of *tariki,* the "other power" that Jodo-sect believers value so highly:

> This is the first time I have used this expression, which suggests the "other power" [of Buddha]. A work that bears its creator's signature is obviously determined by the powers of the individual in question. However, when the object is anonymous, it is the work of many ordinary, unlettered people. If there is beauty here, it does not stem from the power of a single individual, but must be seen as the work of a power surpassing the people involved, operating behind the scenes to endow the object with beauty. To put the matter simply, the other power (*tariki*), the hand of Buddha, is at work in the beauty of the anonymous object. (From *On Buddhist Aesthetics*)

Furthermore, on the subject of *mingei* (folk crafts), Yanagi gives the following five criteria:

> First is that the object be unattributed. Second is that it be the work of a craftsperson. Third is that it be an article of everyday use. Fourth is that it be an article produced in quantity. Fifth is that it is not an article that was made specifically to be beautiful. (From *Things and Religion*)

By this definition, *gassho zukuri* dwellings surely represent the epitome of *mingei*.

There is no record of the date of construction of most individual *gassho zukuri* dwellings, so we don't know exactly when each was built. Of the fifty dwellings I have dismantled to date, only two have been clearly datable. The one from the Naka Ise area of the village of Izumi, which became my own home in Kamakura, dates from 1734. And a dwelling, which I used for the Tagawa residence in Hakone, from Ikeda township in Fukui Prefecture dates from 1804. We can estimate that most *gassho zukuri* buildings were constructed from the middle to the late Edo period, with some newer examples being built at the beginning of the Meiji period (1868–1912).

. . .

The areas where *gassho zukuri* buildings are commonly found are among the few regions in Japan where snow lies on the ground

Rethatching *gassho zukuri* roofs was a communal affair.

ユイによる屋根の葺きかえ風景（白川村）

　合掌造り民家は主に、岐阜県中部および富山県山間部の豪雪地帯に分布している。岐阜県中部に源流をもつ庄川は、御母衣ダム、白川郷、五箇山、庄川村などの秘境を経て、富山湾に注いでいるが、その流域には、合掌造りの村々が点在している。なかでも、白川郷と五箇山の合掌造り民家の集落は観光名所にもなっており、1995年にはユネスコの世界遺産にも登録された。

　白川郷には、倶利伽羅峠で木曾義仲に破れた平家の残党が隠れ住んだという落人伝説がある。まさに陸の孤島のような秘境で、東は飛騨山脈、西は白山に囲まれた山間いの集落だ。土地の9割以上が山林であり、耕作地は非常に小さい。

　この地方は、樹齢の古い良質の木材が豊富なため、江戸時代の一時期には天領（幕府の直轄地）として年貢も木材で納めていた。合掌造り民家の骨組みに使われる杉、欅、松、楢、栗などはもちろん、高級な檜の古木などもあったが、これらは年貢として上納されたり、他の地方に売って金を稼ぐために使われていたようだ。今日でも飛騨地方は、日本で最も林業の盛んな地域の一つである。

　豊富な木材のほか、この地方のもう一つの特色は昔から浄土真宗の門徒が多いことである。それは室町時代の半ばに、本願寺を建立した浄土真宗中興の祖といわれる蓮如聖人（1415〜1499）が、越前吉崎を根拠地として北陸から飛騨地方にかけて精力的に布教を行ったことによる。親鸞を宗祖とする浄土真宗は、一言でいえば、自我のはからいを捨て、すべてを阿弥陀様におまかせしようという「他力本願」の信仰である。この地方の門徒たちはいわゆる葬式仏教ではなく、心からの篤信者なのである。そのため合掌造り民家にはたいてい独立した仏間（ブツマ）があり、現在でも立派な仏壇を備えた家が多い。

　「他力」ということについて、「民芸」運動で知られる柳宗悦（1889〜1961）は、著書の中でこんなことをいっている。

　「私は、"他力的"と云う文字をここで始めて用いるが、在銘品の方は明らかに個人の力量によって左右されているものだが、無銘品の方は、多くの無学な平凡な人たちの仕事であるから、もしそこに美しさがあるとすると、個人の力から湧き出たものでなく、何かかかる人を超えた力が背後に働いて作品を美しくさせていると考えねばなるまい。簡単に云うと、一功の無銘品の美には他力が働いていると云うことになろう」（『仏教美学について』）

for more than four months of the year, regularly achieving a depth of two or three meters (from six to ten feet). The characteristic steep roof of the *gassho zukuri* style is designed to shed snow, and the stables for livestock located within the house proper are intended to protect the animals from the heavy snowfall, reflecting the concept of livestock as part of the family.

In these areas, with their poor soil and limited arable land, slash-and-burn agriculture was common until the Taisho period (1912–26). The fallen leaves of broadleaf trees, such as beech and oak, are rich in nutrients, which make the soil more fertile. These leaves, which would fall in autumn, were burned in May or June of the following year, making an ash-rich "burned" field (*yakihata*). Crops included rice, wheat, millet, chestnuts, potatoes, hemp, and soybeans, but since rice was in short supply, millet was the staple food of everyday life. A mixture of roughly thirty percent rice to seventy percent millet was most common. Other staples included millet—cooked alone—and dumplings made from horse chestnuts. Although horse chestnuts were an important food source, their strong bitter flavor meant that a great deal of time and effort was necessary to leach out the bitterness before they could be eaten. Since the villagers made a barely self-sufficient living under the harsh conditions of the cold climate and limited, poor soil, the custom of mutual help emerged naturally. This tradition survives even today. The communal task of rethatching roofs in Shirakawago village, often seen in television documentaries in Japan, shows the system of cooperation in action. Found in this kind of architectural task, as well as in weddings, funerals and so on, the custom of exchange of labor, with the entire village lending manpower, is known in Naka Ise as *temagae*.

The side business of raising silkworms in the second story of *gassho* houses began around the middle of the Edo period and continued until the early decades of the twentieth century.

The essence of the seasonal lives of these honest villagers wafted unnoticed in the smoke from the sunken hearth; it colored the great central *daikoku-bashira* pillar, staining the bamboo and the curved beams over the course of centuries producing an extraordinary living space. We might say that the passing of time itself creates this beauty. This lies in stark contrast to the contemporary house, which appears bright and functional at first glance, but becomes grimy and unattractive within a few years.

I can't help but think that *gassho zukuri* dwellings silently rebuke our contemporary way of life and conceptions of beauty.

また、「民芸」については、次のような五つの特色をあげている。

「第一は無銘品であること。第二は職人の作である事。第三は実用品である事。第四は多量に出来た品である事。第五は美しさをとりわけ狙って作られたものでないこと」(『物と宗教』)

この定義からすると、合掌造り民家は「民芸」そのものではないだろうか。

一つ一つの合掌造り民家がいつごろ建てられたのかは、どこにも記銘がないのでほとんどわからない。私がこれまで解体した50棟のうち、はっきりしたものはたった2軒しかない。1軒は、私の自宅(鎌倉・源氏山)になっている和泉村中伊勢の野村家で1734年(享保19年)、もう1軒は箱根の田川邸の元になった福井県池田町の民家で、1807年(文化4年)である。江戸時代は1603年(慶長8年)から1867年(慶応3年)までだから、その多くは江戸時代中期から後期にかけて建てられたもので、新しいものでも明治時代の初めと推定できるだろう。

合掌造り民家が多く点在する地域は降雪期間が4ヵ月を越え積雪量も2～3mに達するという有数の豪雪地帯である。合掌造り独特の急勾配の屋根はこの積雪を防ぐための工夫であり、またウマヤ(馬屋)が家の中にあるのは、家畜も家族の一員であるという意識のほかに、豪雪から家畜を守るための知恵だと思われる。

やせた零細な耕地で農業を営まなくてはならなかったこの地域では、大正時代まで焼畑農業が行われていた。ブナ、樫などの広葉樹は落葉の中に土を肥沃にする養分を多く含んでいる。秋にこれらを伐採し、翌年の5、6月ごろに焼いて、焼畑を作る。作物には米、麦、稗、粟、芋、麻、大豆などがあったが、米は不足していたため、日常生活の主食は稗だった。米は2、3割であとは稗という混合飯が主で、ほかに稗だけの稗飯、栃餅などを主食としていた。栃の実も大切な食料の一つだが、苦味が強くアク抜きのために灰汁につけたり小川で漂したりと、食べるまでに大変な手間と日数を要する。このように寒冷な気候、やせて狭い耕地という厳しい条件のもとに自給自足する生活の中で、村民の間には自然に相互扶助の習慣ができあがってきた。これが今でも受け継がれているユイ(結)である。テレビなどでもよく紹介される白川郷の屋根の茅の葺きかえ作業はこの「結」の方式によって共同で行われている。こうした建築活動から冠婚葬祭などに到るまで、集落単位でおたがいに労働力を提供しあう習慣は、テマガエ(労力交換)とよばれている。

建物の二階に蚕棚を作り養蚕を始めたのは江戸時代の半ばごろからで、これは昭和の初めまで続いていた。

四季を通じて篤実な村民の日々の暮らしは、いつしか囲炉裏の煙に溶け込み、大黒柱や天井の煤竹や曲り木の梁を100年、200年と燻し続け、類いまれな居住空間を創りあげていった。長い歳月の「時間」が美を創造したといってよい。一見、機能的で華やかに見えても、数年のうちに汚れて魅力の乏しい建物に変わってしまう現代住宅とは、まさに対極的である。

合掌造り民家は、現代の私たちの生活ぶりや美意識を、無言のうちに痛烈に批判しているように思えてならない。

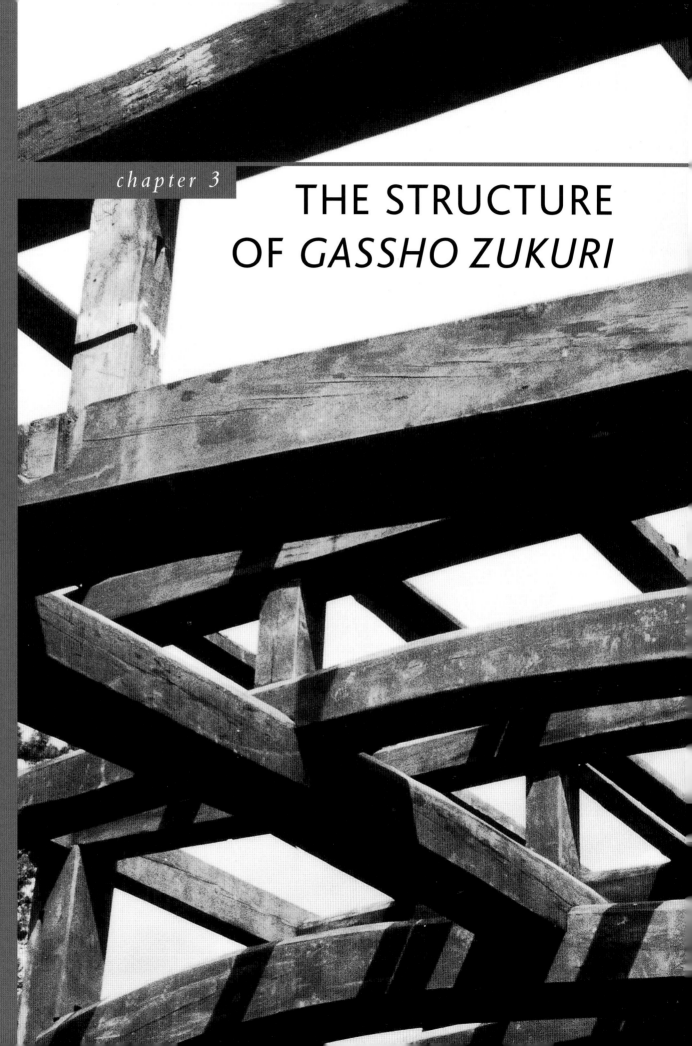

chapter 3

THE STRUCTURE OF *GASSHO ZUKURI*

第3章　私の手がけた合掌造りの構造

Although there are differences in scale, *gassho zukuri* dwellings display similar structures. The design of the structure evolved over time and is not the work of any particular individual.

In addition to the system of communal labor, the services of specialist carpenters were used. Under a system known as *bansho*, which began during the Nara period (710–94), these craftsmen would travel from Hida to the then capital of Nara to assist by turns in building projects. The ground-floor living area of *gassho* houses, with its large, well-engineered columns and beams, was constructed by these carpenters as well, and became known as *banshodate*, or "built by the *bansho*." In contrast, the roof itself was built by the villagers. Because the way the roof beams—logs, actually—connected at the top resemble a pair of thighs, or *mata*, the upper structure came to be known as *matadate*, or "built like thighs." In fact, a similar method of lashing logs together to make a roof, called *tenchikongen miyazukuri*, was used in Japan even during the prehistoric period, and so has been handed down from antiquity.

In a *gassho zukuri* farmhouse, two huge cedar logs are placed together like a pair of hands held palm to palm, fingertips touching in an attitude of prayer (*gassho*). The ends of the logs are sharpened like pencils to a point, called *hozo*, and holes of matching size (*hozo ana*) are carved in the supporting beam. The logs are then fitted into the holes, where they rest without being nailed or fastened down. When both logs have been fitted into the base at an interval of 1 *ken* (about 1.8 meters/6 feet), the distinctive triangular shape of the roof is formed.

Ropes are used to bird the *gassho* rafters to thin slats, or purlins.

Next, bamboo or small tree branches are woven horizontally and vertically to make a lattice, which in turn is tied onto the horizontal slats. Nails are not originally used at all in *gassho zukuri* dwellings. Ropes and the simple mortises and tenons cut into the wood are the only adhesives used.

When all the lattices have been put into place, the roof is finally covered. Bunch after bunch of miscanthus grass (*susuki*) is painstakingly tied onto the lattice. The job is completed when the thatch reaches a thickness of about 30 to 50 centimeters (8 to 13 inches). It should be noted here that no boards of any sort are used on the underside of the roof.

The eaves are constructed with a 1-meter-square (11-foot-square) opening that allows smoke from the hearth to escape

The central pillar and *sashikamoi* beam.

大黒柱に三方からサシカモイがつながる。柱を貫通した長いホゾとそれをとめるクサビが見える。

from the triangular space under the thatched roof. The smoke also helps prevent dampness, rot, and insect damage in the house.

The ground floor *banshodate* section is the living area. The layout of the house from Izumi Village is typical of those in Fukui Prefecture (see the floor plan on page 24).

Traditional Japanese builders use the previously mentioned unit of measurement known as *ken*, about 1.8 meters (6 feet), to determine the placement of columns and so on. This house is 6-*ken* wide (10.8 meters/36 feet) and 4-*ken* deep (7.2 meters/24 feet), which is a typical size. Twelve pillars run through the outer walls at 2-*ken* (3.6- meters/12-foot) intervals. In the center of the house are two central pillars, known respectively as upper and lower. As all these pillars support the weight of the edifice, massive, sturdy timber is selected. Almost all of the pillars, including the outer ones, are made of zelkova.

The house is made up of four spaces: the guest space, called *dei*; the bedroom area, called *nando*; the living and kitchen area, known as *daidoko*; and the earthen-floor area, called *doma*. The house faces south to catch the sun, and has an earthen-floored space at the entrance (also known in this region as *uchi niwa*, literally, "inner garden"), and an *engawa* (a wooden deck running

合掌造りの民家は、その規模に大小はあってもみな似たような構造をもっている。特定の誰かがデザインしたというものではない。

この民家の構造はマタダテ（股建て）とよばれる合掌屋根の上部と、バンショウダテ（番匠建て）とよばれる一階の居住空間になっている下部とで成り立っている。

番匠とは、奈良時代以来、飛騨の国から京に上り交代で普請（工事）を手伝った職人のこと。合掌造りの屋根が村人たちの「ユイ」による共同作業で作られるのに対し、バンショウダテは、専門の職人たちが手がけることからこの名がある。

マタダテ（股建て）は、屋根の組み合わせが股の形に似ていることから、そうよばれているらしい。杉丸太をテントのように組み合わせた、日本の家屋の原型とされる様式テンチコンゲンミヤヅクリ（天地根元宮造り）といわれ、古くから伝えられていた。

合掌造りの屋根の部分は、合掌材とよばれる2本の大きな杉丸太を、拝むとき手を合わせる「合掌」に似た形に組む。そして合掌材の根元の部分は鉛筆を削ったように尖らせてある。これをホゾという。合掌材を受ける桁には、ホゾの大きさに合わせてホゾ穴を彫っておく。合掌材はこのホゾをホゾ穴に突き刺してはあるが、ただ桁に載っているだけであり、固定されていない。一対の合掌材を1間間隔で合掌台に載せていくと、三角形の合掌屋根構造ができあがる。家が大きいときは、桁に直角に一間間隔で合掌台を設け、その両端にホゾ穴をあけ、ここで合掌材を受けるという構造をとっている。

Three massive beams converge.

柱に巨大な梁が三本つながる。

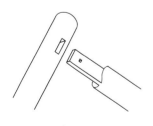

Pegged penetrating tenon.

合掌材の先端のホゾとホゾ穴。2本の杉丸太を組む。

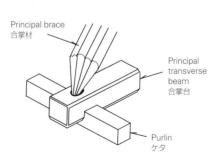

Principal brace
合掌材

Principal transverse beam
合掌台

Purlin
ケタ

Positioning the foot of the brace.

鉛筆のように尖った合掌材の根元。

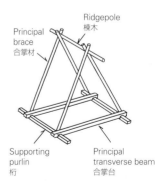

Ridgepole
棟木

Principal brace
合掌材

Supporting purlin
桁

Principal transverse beam
合掌台

Roof structure.

合掌材を合掌台に載せる。

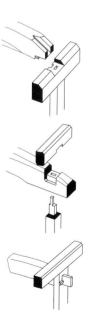

Three types of traditional joints.

いろいろな木組み。

alongside the house), which faces the garden proper (*soto niwa*). Generally, in the modern era, *engawa* are enclosed by glass doors—in other words, inside the house—but, in this region, the *engawa* is situated outside the external wall. When it rains, storm shutters are slid into grooves along the outer edge of the *engawa*, completely enclosing the space and "bringing it inside."

As one comes into the *uchi niwa* from the entrance, the space is surprisingly small. To the right is the stable, and a large wooden-floored room is found where one steps up from the earthen-floored area. This is called the lower *daidoko*. In the far right of the room is a space of less than the size of one tatami mat, called a *kamiya* ("paper maker's"). This is where *washi* (Japanese paper) was made from the bark of the paper mulberry. To the left of this is a scullery, with a sink and draining board made from a large tree laid on its side and hollowed out. A duct constantly carries clean water in from the mountainside, and a drain carries waste water back outside. There were also shelves for storing eating utensils and a space for storing food.

When all is said and done, however, the main focus of the house is the sunken *irori* hearth in the middle of the room. The hearth was not solely for cooking; it was also a source of heat and the place where people gathered to eat—a place of communication. To the left of the lower kitchen is the upper *daidoko*. Here, too, is a hearth, though it is used only for special occasions. These two broad spaces, which were simply called *daidoko*, were places for meals and for working in the evening. To put it in today's terms, the *daidoko* area served as the common room for the family, the effective heart of the house.

Rooms used every day, such as this big room and the earthen-floored space, which are are called *ke* spaces, in contrast to the *hare* areas used for receiving guests, weddings, funerals, and other formal or special occasions. In this region, the *hare* rooms are called *dei* rooms. The term *dei* is said to derive from the expression *o-deisama*, which signified the master of a house of the nobility. In the *dei* room were a *tokonoma* alcove, the altar, and display shelves. In the humble tatami-floored *gassho zukuri* dwelling, it was an unusually elegant room. The ceiling of the *dei* room is low, at about 2.7 meters (9 feet), and the heavy, rough-hewn beams are concealed behind it. It is an unusual room in that smoke cannot get in as in the *ke* rooms, the ceiling being made of boards rather than the *susudake* bamboo found in the rest of the house. The room is clearly partitioned by doors of wood and *karakami* printed paper.

At the time of the summer Bon Festival and other occasions when a priest came to recite sutras, it was the custom for him to go directly into the *dei* room, where the altar was, via the *engawa* deck, without passing through the *ke* rooms.

As one enters the main space from the low entranceway, the first surprise is the exceptionally high ceiling. Compared with a normal Japanese house, with a ceiling of about 2.7 meters (9 feet), it has a height of about 4 meters (13 feet). About 1 meter (3 1/4 feet) below the ceiling, thick, curved beams, just large enough to get one's arms around, run horizontally, intersecting at each pillar. Pliant pinewood with plenty of resin is used for these beams. The way they curve, unique to pine, is also a natural virtue, resulting from the ability of the tree to survive under the weight of harsh winter snow.

Another feature is the device called the *sashikamoi*. This is a piece of wood, also made of pliant pine, about 30 or 40 centimeters wide (12 to 16 inches), which connects pillar to pillar at a height of about 1.75 meters (5 1/2 feet) above the floor. The standard *kamoi* serves, in combination with the *shikii* groove below, as the rails for wooden or paper sliding doors. Naturally, the *sashikamoi* also plays the role of a rail in some places, but, together with the pillars with which it is connected, it also carries the burden of supporting the heavy *gassho zukuri* roof. If there were no *sashikamoi*, it would be necessary to have many more pillars to spread the load. It plays an indispensable role in creating a comfortable living space.

Seeing the broad beams of curving timber alone, one might say they make a forceful, imposing impression. Yet the ancient pillars, beams, and *sashikamoi* within this wide space, measuring 4 meters (13 feet) from the floor, seem to emit an aura of soothing tranquillity. This sense is reinforced by the ceiling. The high ceiling is covered, not by boards, but by bamboo. On looking closely, one can see that the bamboo canes laid neatly into the rectangular space of the ceiling as reinforcement are of different thicknesses, and that over long years they have been stained by

A standard *minka* floor plan.

標準的な民家の間取り（和泉村史より）

ここで縄が登場する。合掌材の外側に直径10cmほどの横木を縄で縛りつけるのである。この横木を水平に60cm間隔で、何本か縛りつける。

次に竹や細い木の枝を縦、横に組んだ格子を作り、さらに横木に縄で縛りつける。合掌造り民家では、釘は一切使われない。素材を結びつける手段は、この縄と、木を削って作る「ホゾ」や「ホゾ穴」による結合という素朴な方法だけである。

格子が横木にすべて縛りつけられると、いよいよ屋根葺きにかかる。茅のひと束ひと束を格子に丹念に縄で縛りつけていき、厚さが30cmから50cmになると完成である。ここで注目すべきことは、屋根裏には板のようなものは一切使われていないということだ。

茅葺き屋根の下の三角形の空間に囲炉裏の煙が充満すると、妻側に空けられた1m四方の窓から外に流れ出ていくという仕組みになっている。この煙も家の除湿、防虫、防腐などに役立っているのである。

一階の「番匠建て」の部分は居住空間である。私にとってなじみ深い福井県和泉村の民家の標準的な間取りは、24ページの図のようになっている。

間口6間、奥行4間というのが標準で、主たる柱は2間間隔で12本である。

家の中心部には2本の大黒柱があり、カミ（上）大黒柱、シモ（下）大黒柱とよばれている。この大黒柱は建物の重量を支えるためのもので、太くて堅牢な木材が選ばれる。外周のものも含めて、柱はほとんど欅である。

間取りは、大きく分けるとデイとよばれる客間、ナンドとよばれる寝室、ダイドコとよばれる居間兼台所、そして土間の四つに区切られている。

家は日あたりの良い南向きに建てられ、入口土間（ウチニワともいう）や縁側などがあり、縁側はソトニワ（外庭）に面している。普通縁側といえばガラス戸の内側、つまり家の内部にあるが、この地方では縁側は家の板壁の外側にある。雨のときは、雨戸をたてて内側に取り込むようになっている。

入口からウチニワ（土間）に入ると、ここは意外に狭い。右側にウマヤがあり、土間を上がったところに板敷の広間がある。ここを下ダイドコという。部屋の右奥には、畳一畳足らずのカミヤ（紙漉場）がある。ここではコウゾで和紙が作られていた。その左側に水屋とよばれる台所仕事のための流しがあり、ここには大きな木を横にくり抜いた流しがある。山のほうから樋を伝って常時、清水が流れ込み、また樋で屋外に排出されるようになっている。下ダイドコには食器などを入れる棚も、食べものを貯蔵するスペースも備わっている。しかし、なんといっても主役は、部屋の真中にある囲炉裏である。囲炉裏は単に炊事をするだけでなく、暖房装置であり、またここに集って食事をしたりするコミュニケーションの場でもある。下ダイドコの左側に上ダイドコがありここにも囲炉裏があるが、この囲炉裏は行事のときの暖房用で平素はもっぱら下ダイドコの囲炉裏を使用した。ダイドコとよばれるこの二つの広間は、食事や夜なべ仕事などをする場所だが、今風にいえ

ば、一家団らんの間というか実質的には家の中心といってよい。

このように、日常的に使われる土間や広間を「ケ」というのに対し、冠婚葬祭や接客などあらたまった特別の時に使われる間は「ハレ」という。この地方ではこの「ハレ」の間を「デイ」の間とよぶ。「デイ」とは公家の主人を「御出居様」とよんだのが語源らしい。デイの間には床の間、仏壇、飾棚などがあり、合掌造り民家の中では、例外的にエレガントな畳敷の空間である。天井が2m70cm程度と低く、重くいかつい曲り木の梁などは天井裏に隠されている。ケの空間のように煙が来ない例外的な空間になっているので、天井も媒竹ではなく板である。部屋は唐紙や板戸などできちんと仕切られている。お盆など読経のためにお坊さんがやって来るときなどは、ケの間を通らず縁側から直接、仏壇のあるデイの間に行くのが習慣であった。

建物に入ってまず驚くのは、天井が非常に高いことだ。普通の和風家屋の天井が2m70cm程度なのに対し、4mほどの高さがある。天井から1mほど下がったところに、一抱えもあるような、太く曲った梁が、縦横に縫うように交差して柱に到る。この梁には材料として樹脂の多いねばりのある松材が使われている。あの曲り具合も、幾冬もの厳しい雪を生き延びた自然の成せる業で、松独特のものであろう。

もう一つ、サシカモイ（差鴨居）というものを取りいれた工夫がある。差鴨居は床上1m75cmぐらいの高さで柱と柱を連結する

The curved beams (shaded in the structure below) of the *minka* were harvested from trees growing on steep slopes.

山の急斜面で風雪に耐えて育った曲がり木。これを力学的に生かし民家に利用。

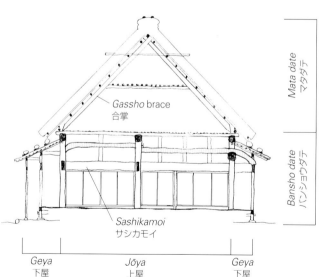

Basic structural elements of the *minka*. (This illustration shows the original structure used for the Roderick House.)

旧野村家断面図（穴馬郷中伊勢）

the smoke from the hearth to a tawny caramel color. This smoke-stained bamboo, called *susudake*, develops a lovely patina over time and is now much prized as a material for the bamboo ladles and flower baskets used in the tea ceremony. If one climbs up into the roof space, one finds that woven straw mats have been laid over the bamboo lattice. Although the perimeter of the living area of *gassho zukuri* dwellings (the *banshodate* section) is enclosed with boarded walls, no planked flooring of any kind is used to separate stories, from the lowermost floor all the way up to the thatch of the roof.

Firewood is burned in the hearth in the living area all year. Its smoke darkens the pillars, beams, and *sashikamoi*, colors the *susudake* beautifully, and climbs up to pass through the straw mats into the triangular "praying hands" space. Finally, it permeates the thatch to reach the outside air. Over time, the smoke from the hearth not only has the virtue of preserving beams and pillars, it also has such practical functions as preventing dampness, conserving the foodstuffs kept for that purpose on the *hiama* shelf hung over the fire, and protecting the thatched roof and the straw mats under it from insects, as well as allowing air to travel from the floor to the roof. All of these benefits attributed to the hearth smoke and the use of an open bamboo lattice, in turn contribute to lengthening the house's life span.

Another characteristic of the *gassho zukuri* dwelling is its pliable structure (*ju-kozo*). It is surprising that the *gassho zukuri* roof is mainly held in place on top of the lower frame by gravity. In storms, the roof may become deformed or shift slightly, but this is no cause for alarm. It resettles naturally, since the tenons are forced back into their mortises by the weight of the roof itself. This is similar to the way the upper sections of contemporary Japanese high-rise buildings are allowed to sway to absorb earthquake tremors.

In 1935, a book by the well-known German architect Bruno Taut (1880–1938) was published in Japan under the title *Nihonbi no saihakken* (Rediscovery of Japanese Beauty), and became a best-seller. In the book, Taut heaped praise on *gassho zukuri* farmhouses of Shirakawa, as well as the more famous Katsura Detached Palace in Kyoto. He commented that the functional and logical structure of the farmhouses was without parallel anywhere in Japan.

These practical houses, made only from wood, rope, and thatch, can truly be said to be masterworks, the product of the applied wisdom of generations of villagers, dating back to the days of the master carpenters of Edo-period (1600–1868) Hida.

幅30〜40cm位の横木である。これも材料はねばりのある松が使われている。普通鴨居といえば敷居と上下一体で唐紙や引戸のレールの役目を果たしている。もちろん差鴨居も場所によってはレールの役目を果たすが、連結している柱とともに、重い合掌造りの屋根を支える力仕事を請負っている。もし差鴨居がなければ、力を分散させるため、もっと数多くの柱が必要となる。住みやすい空間を創り上げるうえで必須の役割を担っているのである。

曲り木の太い梁など、それだけを見れば豪壮という言葉がぴったりに思える。だが、古びた柱や梁、差鴨居は、床上4mの広い空間の中で、心がやすらぐ静謐ともいえる雰囲気を辺りに発散しているように感じられる。

このことをさらに実感させるのは天井である。高い天井を覆うのは板ではなく竹である。天井の補強材で矩形に仕切られたスペースに竹がきれいに敷き詰められているが、よく見れば竹の太さは不揃いで、長い歳月を経て囲炉裏の煙で燻され茶褐色のあめ色をした煤竹となっている。この美しさはちょっと例えようがない。煤竹は今では貴重品で、茶道で使われる茶杓や花籠などの原材料として珍重されている。上にのぼって天井裏から見ると、この煤竹の簀子の上には筵が一面に敷かれている。合掌造り民家では、住居空間である番匠建ての周囲は板壁で囲まれているが、台所の床から屋根の茅葺きまで階を仕切る床材としては、一切板は使われていない。

住居部分にある囲炉裏は四季を通じて薪が燃やされる。その煙は柱や梁や差鴨居を燻し、煤竹を美しく着色し、上にのぼって筵を通り三角の合掌部分に達する。最後は屋根の茅葺きの中に浸透して外気と通じる。この間、囲炉裏の煙は、これまで経てきた長い時間、梁や柱に功徳を施すだけでなく、湿気を取り除き、囲炉裏の上につるされたヒアマ（火天）上に置いてある保存食の腐食を防ぎ、天井裏の筵や茅葺き屋根の防虫の役目を果たすという実用的な機能ももっている。床から屋根まで空気が通じている構造と相まって、家を長もちさせる役割を果している。

このほか、合掌造り民家の特徴として「柔構造」があげられる。これは驚くべきことだが、合掌造りの屋根は、番匠建ての柱で支えられている桁の上にただ載っているだけなのである。嵐のときなどは、大きく揺れるが、恐れる必要はない。合掌屋根自体の重みで、ホゾがホゾ穴に自然にめり込んで復元するようになっている。現代の高層ビルが、地震のとき、地上部分を大きく揺らすことによって振動を吸収し安全を保つのに似ている。

木と縄と茅だけを素材にしたこの合理的な民家は、飛騨の匠以来、村民たちの智恵が集積されてできあがった傑作といってよいだろう。

戦前の1939年に、ドイツの建築学者ブルーノ・タウトの『日本美の再発見』が岩波書店から発行され話題になったことがある。タウトはこの本の中で、日本の代表的建築美として、桂離宮とともに白川郷の合掌造り民家をあげている。彼はその中で「その構造が合理的であり論理的であるという点においては、日本全国をつうじてまったく独特の存在である」と書いている。

chapter 4

RENEWING OLD DWELLINGS

RIGHT: The appeal of the traditional Japanese farmhouse is apparent in this photo of the Takishita House. Massive hand-hewn beams, which are carefully fitted together, protect the expansive space beneath and age beautifully over the years.

中二階から居間を見下ろす。力強い太い梁は民家の特徴。

The transfer of a *minka* dwelling to a new location involves the dismantling of the beams and pillars of the house's basic frame and its reassembly at the new site, just as it was. These physical elements themselves are extremely important and cannot by replaced by other timber. In particular, the subtle arcs of the naturally curved timbers, which are so skillfully incorporated into the wooden frame, are all one-of-a-kind, and when they are reassembled, a wonderful two-hundred-year-old space comes back to life. Even if one were to collect other old timbers and construct a similar space, it would still lack the authentic flavor of a historic folk dwelling. The spiritual values of the original builders and residents—the villagers who lived as one with nature—would not be felt in the same way. It is my belief that having a sure grasp of the space created by the pillars and beams of the base frame is the most important part of the art of moving and converting a *minka* (*minka ichiku*).

Since nails and adhesives are not used in old *minka* dwellings, one can, in theory, take the houses apart and reassemble them over and over again once the joints have been loosened. The position of the pillars within the basic structure imposes restrictions on the floor plan. However, it is possible to remove secondary pillars and walls, and the structure lends itself easily to other uses and functions. As a result, one need not be constrained by the original usage: a bold plan, suited to the environment and circumstances of the new site, is entirely possible. A conceptual conversion can be done, one that would have been unthinkable at the original village site. Naturally, in such instances the exterior and the layout of the rooms also change.

When one is planning the transfer and conversion of a *minka* dwelling, the harmony of old and new, Japanese and Western, practical and aesthetic must not be forgotten. There is no single right answer in this matter, being very much a problem of individual taste. To ensure comfortable living conditions, the builder must incorporate plumbing, air conditioning, soundproofing, insulation, and other modern conveniences in a structure where they were previously absent. On the other hand, apparently impractical indirect lighting and lamps with paper shades are also desirable devices for making effective use of the space of the dwelling. The *minka* has contemporary value only when a beautiful space is created, one that possesses not only comfort but also a harmony between the original and new elements.

The transfer and reconstruction of such dwellings is expensive and time-consuming, and demands a great deal of love and patience. But the house rewards such effort and sensitivity with an even greater sense of worth and satisfaction.

民家の移築とは、基本構造の柱と梁の軸組をそっくり移すことである。これらの柱や梁はたいへん重要で、ほかの木材と取りかえられない。とくに自然の曲り木など微妙なカーブを上手に取りこんだ木組は、自然界に二つとない。このオリジナルの柱と梁が移築されて再び200年前の不思議な空間が甦る。もしただの古材を集めて似たような空間を作ったとしても、それは、平成の時代の空間で、古民家の空間とはほど遠い異なったものである。自然と共生した村人たちの精神性などは伝わってこない。民家の移築再生でもっとも大切なことは、軸組の柱と梁が作りだす空間をよく見極めることにあると私は思う。

民家は釘や接着剤を使用していないので、仕口の栓を抜けば、理論上何度でも解体、組立てが可能である。基本構造に含まれる柱の位置は平面計画に制約を与える。しかし、そのほか従属的な柱は、外したり壁を撤去したりすることができる。異なった用途や機能に対応しやすい仕組みをもっている。だから新天地において過去の用途にこだわらないで、新しい環境と条件に適合する思いきった自由な設計が可能となる。以前所在した村では考えられないような、発想の転換も可能となる。当然、外観も間取りも変わってくる。

移築の設計で忘れてはならないことは、新しい部分と古い部分の調和である。それは、和と洋、合理性と非合理性とのバランスをうまくとることである。これには正確な答えはなく、個人的な感覚の問題である。快適に住むための水回りや空調などの諸設備、防音、断熱など近代的な合理性を取りいれる。一方、非合理的と思われる間接照明や行灯などを使い、民家の空間を効果的に生かす工夫も必要である。快適であり、かつ新旧の調和がとれた美しい空間を作ってこそ、民家の現代的価値が生まれる。

民家の移築には、思いのほかお金と時間がかかり、愛情と忍耐もたくさん必要である。しかし、結果的にはそれに応える、否、それ以上の価値と満足感をもたらしてくれる。

THE RODERICK HOUSE

A wall of sliding glass doors allows a traditional *minka* both light and a view

Let us look at how a *gassho zukuri* dwelling is relocated and reconstructed, using the home of my foster father, John Roderick, as a specific example. This building has a superb location on a hill in Kamakura. On one side is a view of the old town of Kamakura and the ocean at Yuigahama, with the seaside at Zushi being visible at the left. Here, as previously mentioned, we rebuilt the home of the Nomura family, which we had moved from the village of Izumi in Fukui.

The entrance of the Nomura House originally faced south, but at the time of reconstruction, we rotated the entire building one hundred and eighty degrees, so that it faced north. We combined the upper and lower *daidoko* (kitchens) into a joint living and dining room, and allowed it to open to the south to take advantage of the ocean view. As mentioned before, the kitchen was a *ke* (daily life) space, for sitting around the hearth at meals or doing chores in the evening—an everyday space, constantly smoky. In the case of the Nomura House, the upper and lower *daidoko* each had sunken hearths; and these—with the entrance, earthen-floored hall, and the stable off to the left—together constituted this everyday *ke* space. The characteristic of this space was the particular atmosphere it had acquired over decades, during which the beams and pillars had been slowly cured by the smoke. Furthermore, when one considers the size of this *ke* space, one clearly sees it is several times more spacious than the *hare* (ceremonial) area of the *dei* (guest) rooms. In reconstructing the Nomura House, we transformed the *ke* space into *hare* space to make the living and drawing room.

The old *dei* guest areas and the altar room became a modern dining room, kitchen, and bathroom, meaning that what was the ceremonial *hare* space for the Nomura household has been metamorphosed into an everyday *ke* section. The *ke* and *hare* spaces have been fully reversed. This method of inversion has proven extremely efficient for reconstructing *gassho zukuri* dwellings. In around eighty percent of the houses I have handled until now, the everyday *ke* spaces have been changed to a spacious living and drawing room, and the *hare* sections (namely the altar room or drawing room, guest rooms, and so on) have been transformed into kitchens and bathrooms. You might say that this inversion has become the standard layout for the reconstructions I supervise.

The ceiling of the living room of the Roderick House is completely covered with *susudake* bamboo, and the room is enclosed by glass doors all along its south side. Sitting in the room, one gets a view of the distant Zushi marina. The dignity of the beams and pillars, borne of two-hundred-and-fifty years of history, is juxtaposed with the modern light streaming through the glass doors. The odd harmony of these two elements creates a unique living space, spacious yet strangely calming. In the evenings, the paper-shaded lamp in one corner emits a reddish light, creating an indescribably peaceful ambience.

The second floor is reached by a long open staircase on one side of the spacious living room. The second floor is now used as a storehouse for my collection of traditional screens.

For the roof, I don't use thatch at all—present fire codes restrict its use—and as heavy, traditional ceramic tiles (*kawara*) are not usable on such a steep incline, I generally use roofing slate. If the budget allows, I think copper roofing is the best, since the verdigris that develops over the years gives the roof the flavor of an old shrine.

ローデリック邸
相模湾を見おろすリビングに8枚のガラス戸

　合掌造り民家の移築、再生がどのように行われるかをロデリック邸の場合を例にとって具体的に見てみよう。鎌倉の源氏山という高台で、旧鎌倉の市街や由比ヶ浜の海、左方に逗子の海が見える絶好の地が建築予定地である。ここへかつて手に入れた野村家を移築するのである。

　野村家は南側に入口があったが、移築の際それを北側にもってきた（34ページ図参照）。下ダイドコと上ダイドコをワンルームのリビング兼ダイニングルームとし、南に向かって海を眺めるよう開放的にした。つまり元の建物を180度回転したのである。前述のとおり、ダイドコというのはふだん使われる「ケ」の空間で、囲炉裏を囲んで食事をしたり夜なべ仕事をしたりする日常的な場所である。野村家の場合、下ダイドコ、上ダイドコそれぞれに囲炉裏があり、それに入口、土間とその右側にあったウマヤを含めて「ケ」の空間ができあがっていた。この空間の特徴は、長年にわたり梁や柱や差鴨居などが囲炉裏からの煙でじっくり燻されて独特の雰囲気を醸しだしていることだ。また、その広さを見ると冠婚葬祭や接客のための「ハレ」の空間であるデイの間などより数倍も広い。この「ケ」の空間を「ハレ」のスペースに変えたのである。

　デイの間や仏間は、ここでは現代の台所、ダイニングキッチンとなり、浴室になった。野村家では「ハレ」の部分だったスペースが「ケ」の空間として甦ったのである。「ハレ」と「ケ」の逆転の発想である。この逆転の発想は、合掌造りの民家を移築再生する場合、非常に合理的である。私が今まで手がけた家の8割近くは、「ケ」の部分が広いリビングルームや応接間に変わり、「ハレ」の部分、つまりデイの間、仏間等がキッチン、浴室に変身した。いってみれば私の民家移築の際の間取りの定番である。

　ロデリック邸のリビングの天井は煤竹を一面に張り、リビング南側は全面ガラス戸になっており、部屋に座っていながら逗子マリーナまで遠望することができる。250年の歳月を経てすっかり貫禄をつけた梁や柱が醸しだす静謐感と、大きなガラス戸から入ってくる現代的な湘南の光。この二つが奇妙に調和して開放的ながらも不思議に落ち着きが得られ、独得な居住空間を形づくっている。夜には部屋の片隅に置かれた行灯が少し赤みをおびた光を放ち、なんともいえない落ち着いた雰囲気を醸しだす。

　二階へは、広いリビングルームの隅から長いむき出しの階段でのぼる。二階は私の屏風コレクション収納室として使っている。

　屋根については、茅は一切使わず、また急勾配で瓦もその重さのため使用不可能なので、一般的にスレートを使用している。金に糸目をつけなければ銅葺きなど最高だと思う。銅葺きは時が経つと緑青がわいてきて、古い神社の屋根のような趣きがでるからだ。

Old *gassho zukuri* houses are made suitable for contemporary life through subtle modifications. In this case, the screens which divided the inner room from the main space have been removed, and an antique folding screen has been mounted on a wall where sliding doors once stood. The result is a relaxing and contemplative space.

黒光りのする梁、昔の床板、時代屏風、仏像などが、たがいに不思議な調和を醸しだしている一階居間。

Every attempt is made to bring light into the interior of a renovated house, sometimes with spectacular results, as this view shows. The landscape becomes an important part of the house.

居間の南面は全面がガラス窓で、木製のベランダにつながり、みごとな眺めを取り込む。

MAIN FLOOR—ORIGINAL

MAIN FLOOR—RENOVATED

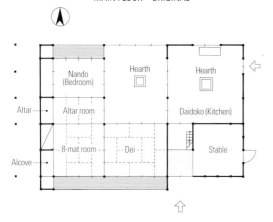

Nando (Bedroom)

Hearth

Hearth

Altar

Altar room

Daidoko (Kitchen)

Alcove

8-mat room

Dei

Stable

UP

DN

Utility

Bath

Alcove

Kitchen

Closet

8-mat room

Entry

Alcove

Utility

Study

Bath

Bedroom

Living area

8-mat room

Storage

UP

Deck

Taken from original 移築部分

COUNTERCLOCKWISE, FROM FAR LEFT: In the Roderick House, the entryway vestibule was left in its original location and retains its vintage flavor.

A deck was added to allow the occupants to enjoy the view.

A constant theme in these renovated *gassho zukuri* houses is the blend of old and new, East and West. The clock on the wall is in fact a traditional touch.

The delicate, tatami-matted room was once a stable.

This view from the small room, which opens to the main living space, shows how light from a garden outside can enhance an intimate space.

A fully modern kitchen was installed in what was formerly the guest-room area.

左上：昔の趣きを残す玄関。左下：遠く相模湾を見おろすベランダ。中：居間東側。天井の梁がアクセントになっている。右上：明るく広々としたキッチン。ふだんの食事にはこの部屋が使われる。右中：もとデイだった玄関の東側の部屋は、畳を取り外して居間につながった空間にしてある。右手の中抜き障子の奥はキッチンと浴室。右下：居間の北側に作られた八畳の和室はもとウマヤだった。右手の中抜き障子は玄関につながっている。

LEFT: A formal dining area suitable for entertaining important guests can easily be incorporated into a renovated *gassho zukuri*.

ABOVE: These stairs to the private rooms above are derived from a Japanese farmhouse ladder.

左：居間東側のダイニングコーナー。あらたまった食事やパーティーのときに使われる。上：居間東端の二階に続く階段。梯子をすこし進化させたような簡素なデザイン。

The second floor is devoted to folding-screen storage space and bedrooms. The guest bedroom is at the far end, and a small study nook lies to the right.

二階の屏風収納室。奥の部屋は客室。右手の本棚は階段の周囲に設けられ、ちょっとした書斎風のコーナーになっている。

SECOND FLOOR

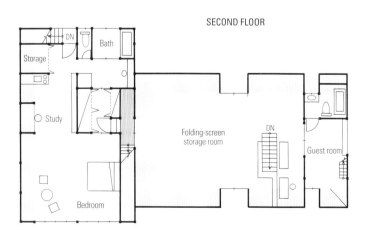

Storage

DN

Bath

Study

Folding-screen
storage room

DN

Guest room

Bedroom

CLOCKWISE, FROM TOP LEFT: The guest room and its bath.

A dignified display alcove has been integrated into the stairwell.

The sink area of the third-floor tearoom.

The third floor has been fitted in the teahouse style. The stairwell is visible through the round window.

左上：二階客室からバスルームを見る。右上：二階から三階に上がる階段室のコーナーを飾り床に。左下：三階屋根裏に作った茶室風の部屋。丸窓の下は階段の吹抜け部分。右下：屋根裏の茶室につなげて右手の小さな障子窓の中に水屋をおさめた。

THIRD FLOOR

6-mat room

6-mat room

THE TAKISHITA HOUSE
A model house in *gassho zukuri* style

When seen from the outside, the Takishita House (West Gallery), which is near the Roderick House, does not appear very large, but as one steps inside, it feels un-expectedly spacious. As usual, the living room was made by combining the upper and lower *daidoko* and the stable, in this case making a space of some 50 mats in area, with a soaring 4-meter (13-foot) ceiling. A large fireplace is set into the wall on the east side of the living room, in front of which is a table made from the door of an old *kura* storehouse building, with a few black leather chairs placed around it.

The approach to the Takishita House is through a traditional garden and gate.

ヨーロッパの田舎家を思わせる外観。

The great feeling of space lent this area is characteristic of *gassho zukuri*. How-ever, since from the outset I intended this building to be a display area for var-ious antiques, I did not apply the con-cept of the inversion of *ke* and *hare* spaces directly. The *dei* room, a formal space set off from the living room, is where screens and such are displayed. This room has been left open, without sliding doors (*fusuma*). A mezzanine floor has been constructed above the *dei* room and kitchen, and the expan-sive living room, as seen from above through small windows, is truly splen-did. This building has four stories. On the uppermost floor, I made a small, tri-angularly roofed private space. A view of Mount Fuji, gradually darkening in the light of the setting sun, is a main attraction of this room. Since warm air rises, this is a cozy little paradise in winter. The triangular roof structure, which forms the upper part of this space, is not necessarily very practical for a living area. However, as a place for a moon-viewing platform, lounging, reading, or some other leisure pursuit, it has great possibilities.

An arrangement of rooms similar to that of the West Gallery, where an occa-sional room, including a *tokonoma* alcove, maintains a formal aura, is also appealing. A sunken *irori* hearth, instead of a fireplace, is also provided. I have built *irori* in five of the houses I have worked on.

The living room, seen from the mezzanine level windows, shows its main features to good advantage: fireplace, mat floor, a table made from a storehouse door, and leather-covered English Victorian chairs.

中二階から見おろした居間。イギリス製の黒皮の椅子に蔵の扉を使ったテーブルを配して。

瀧下邸／ハウス・オブ・アンティックス、ウェストギャラリー

合掌造りの構造がひと目でわかるモデルハウス

　ウェストギャラリー（瀧下邸）は、外観はさほど大きく見えないが、一歩中に入るとその空間は意外に大きく感じる。例にもれず下ダイドコと上ダイドコ、馬屋を一つにしたリビングルームは約50畳ほどの広さで、しかも天井の高さは4ｍ。この広々と感じさせる空間は合掌造りなればこそのものである。東側の壁には大きな暖炉がある。その前には昔の蔵の扉で作ったテーブルがあり、イギリス製の黒皮の椅子がいくつか置いてある。さまざまな骨董品の展示を目的に建てられたこの建物には、「ハレ」と「ケ」の逆転の発想はそのまま適用されていない。リビングルームに隣接した「ハレ」のデイの間は建具を使わず開放し、屏風などが飾ってある。デイの間とキッチンの上には中二階が作られ、ここから見おろすリビングの広々とした眺めもまた、なかなか気に入っている。

北側の建物は4層構造で、最上階の屋根裏には三角形をした狭いプライベートなスペースを作った。富士山が西陽の中で徐々に黒々と変化するのを見ることができるのも、この場所の特徴である。暖気は上方に集まるので、冬などぽかぽかと極楽になる。この上層部は三角屋根の下のため、住空間としてはあまり実用的でないかもしれないが、月見台を作ったりごろんと横になって本を読むなど遊びのスペースとしての利用価値は捨て難い。

　このウェストギャラリーのように、デイの間をそのまま「ハレ」の場として床の間のある部屋にするという間取りも魅力がある。また暖炉のかわりに囲炉裏を作るのも楽しい。私の手がけた家では5軒の家に囲炉裏を作った。

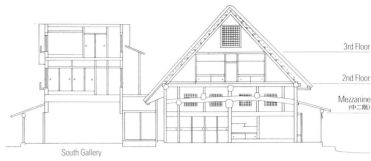

3rd Floor

2nd Floor

Mezzanine
(中二階)

South Gallery

MAIN FLOOR

South Gallery

Office

Bath

Kitchen

10-mat room

Lounge

Alcove

Living area

Bamboo
garden

Entry

Fireplace

Entry

Taken from original 移築部分

FAR LEFT: The fireplace is a foreign element which nonetheless can be handsomely integrated into an old Japanese farmhouse, often with decorative shelves flanking it, as here.

LEFT: The large living area opens to a traditional room where painted screens can be beautifully displayed. The windows of the mezzanine are visible above.

ABOVE: The north side of the house features a traditional veranda opening onto a bamboo garden.

左:一階居間の中心となる暖炉コーナー。暖炉の左右には飾り棚を作った。中:居間につながる十畳の座敷。北側に書院を作った。この部屋の上は中二階となっている。右:廊下の北側の竹林は訪れる人々にたいへん好評である。

ABOVE: Northern light is best for highlighting the outlines of decorative objects. Here, natural northern light is combined with the warm, artificial light of a traditional lantern.

RIGHT: The high ceiling and the effect of the curved beams of the Takishita House can be easily grasped in this view. A traditional Shinto household shrine is mounted high on the wall to the left.

上：障子を通して入る北側からの自然の明かりが穏やかな照明効果になっている。右：天井が高くゆったりした空間。い草マット、太い梁、柱が落ちついた静けさを演出する。音響効果が良いので音楽鑑賞に最適である。

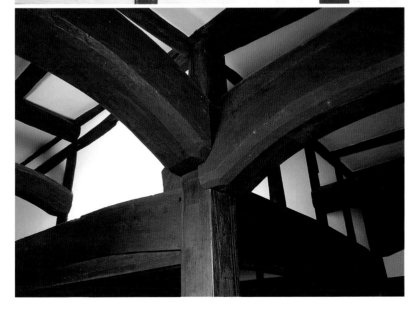

CLOCKWISE, FROM FAR LEFT: The structure of the *gassho zukuri* farmhouse is the product of centuries of evolution. Above the large *o-bari* beams lies a network of smaller beams. The ceiling is made of rush, laid between the small beams.

This particular ceiling treatment involves traditional white plaster spread over the top of the rush and allowed to protrude through.

The *susu-take* treatment uses bamboo, which ages beautifully.

Sometimes ceilings are simply covered with smooth white plaster.

左：古色をつけたよしずの天井。上：豪快な梁組。よしずに漆喰。中：煤竹の天井。下：白漆喰の天井。

CEILINGS: The traditional *gassho zukuri minka* roof is rustic and unkempt, and constant maintenance is required to keep the thatch in place. It is also a great fire hazard. Thus, despite the romantic beauty of the old *minka* roofs, *gassho zukuri* houses require new roofs to replace their thatch. But even when this is done, the details visible from the interior—the original crossed beams, binding ropes, and so forth—should be preserved for their decorative effect. A new ceiling made from bamboo, or reeds covered with plaster, is attractive and clean and retains the atmosphere of a traditional *minka*. The use of whitewash on the ceiling instead of bamboo gives a bright, slightly Western-style effect that is also harmonious.

天井：合掌民家の屋根裏は茅がむきだしで荒々しいので、新しい屋根裏天井を作る必要がある。そのとき、合掌材や巻き縄は装飾的な効果もあるのでぜひ残しておきたい。茅に替えて竹やヨシズに漆喰をのせる新しい天井を作ると、漆喰の効果で清潔感のある部屋ができる。合掌材、竹、漆喰、縄の調和が民家の雰囲気を今に伝える。また白漆喰を煤竹の代わりに使えば洋風になり、明るくすることもでき決して違和感がない。

MEZZANINE（中二階）

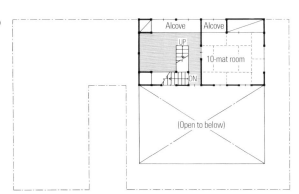

Alcove Alcove

UP

10-mat room

DN

(Open to below)

TOP: The mezzanine level is divided into a room floored with ten tatami mats and a wood-floored gallery space.

BOTTOM: The hard, shiny floor of the gallery space is perfect for showing off large objects such as these ceramic vases. The windows open onto the main living space below.

上：中二階十畳の和室。右手の小窓から吹抜けの居間を見おろすことができる。左下：中二階階段ホールはギャラリーになっていてコレクションが並んでいる。
右下：中二階の階段ホールに江戸期の常滑の瓶。

COUNTERCLOCKWISE, FROM TOP LEFT:

The study area on the western side of the second floor.

The second-floor bedroom.

The rustic stairs to the attic loft.

上：二階書斎の西側。左下：二階の寝室。部屋の凹凸が隠れ家のような雰囲気を作っている。右下：二階の書斎。書棚がいたる所に作られている。屋根裏部屋にのぼる梯子の手すりは屋根下地材を利用している。

LEFT: The triangular space of the loft, which can be used for sleeping, relaxing, or anything else, also makes for warm sleeping quarters for guests.

BELOW: The third-floor of the wing added to the southern end of the Takishita House offers a panoramic view of the ocean.

左：三階の屋根裏部屋は小さな三角形のスペースで、合掌屋根に抱かれた秘密の小部屋のようである。
下：サウスギャラリー三階からの眺望。

THIRD FLOOR

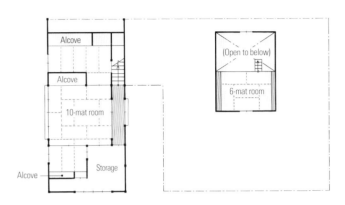

LEFT: The large central pillar is important both structurally and symbolically. It is one of the spiritual centers of the traditional Japanese farmhouse.

BELOW, RIGHT: This *gassho zukuri* house is neatly camouflaged by its New England–style exterior.

左：一階広間。白漆喰の天井と、どっしりした大黒柱の対比が美しい。広々とした空間に畳の部屋がみごとに組み込んである。右：ニューイングランド風外観の玄関。

HOUSE OF ANTIQUES, EAST GALLERY

A Japanese sense of space framed by a Western exterior

Because the East Gallery, known as the House of Antiques, was built in a scenic area with a height restriction of 8 meters (26 feet), making a tall *gassho zukuri* roof impossible, I converted it to a low, two-story building. I have raised the ground on the north slope to catch a view of the ocean. I wanted to display a large quantity of Old Imari pottery at this gallery, so I used the limited land to the fullest, building two stories to provide sufficient display space. I cut the edge of the lower-frame (*banjodate*) section and built a new second floor. Although this gave me space for display, it resulted in a square, boxlike structure without eaves, so I used white siding on the exterior walls to give a New England effect. This is contrived so that visitors, having approached this light, modern entrance, are surprised when the door is opened. Massive, bulky, blackened beams from an old *minka* run overhead, and thick pillars support the ceiling. The *dei* room also opens out, a spacious room covered with tatami mats. Commenting on this contrast between the New England–style exterior and the reconstructed interior of an Edo-period (1600–1868) dwelling, people have called this gallery the "surprise house."

ハウス・オブ・アンティックス、イーストギャラリー
四角いボックスの内部に和風空間

　風致地区に建つイーストギャラリーは、8mの高さ制限があり、合掌屋根にはできないため、低い総二階建てにした。北斜面の地盤を高くして海が見えるようにしている。このギャラリーには、古伊万里をたくさん展示したかったので、ショースペースを確保するため、限られた土地をめいっぱい使って総二階にすることにした。番匠建てのひさしの部分をカットし、二階は新しく継ぎ足した。これで展示のためのスペースは確保したが、結果的に軒のない四角い箱のようなものになってしまったので、外壁に白いサイディングを用いニューイングランド風にした。来訪された方々はこのモダンで軽い入口の辺りを眺めながら、ドアを開けると、アッと驚く仕掛けになっているのである。中にはドッシリと重く黒ずんだ梁が走り、太い柱が天井を支えている。デイの間も畳の広間としてそこに広がっている。ニューイングランド風な外観と江戸時代の日本の民家を再現した内部。このギャップを評して、人々はこのギャラリーをビックリハウスとよぶ。

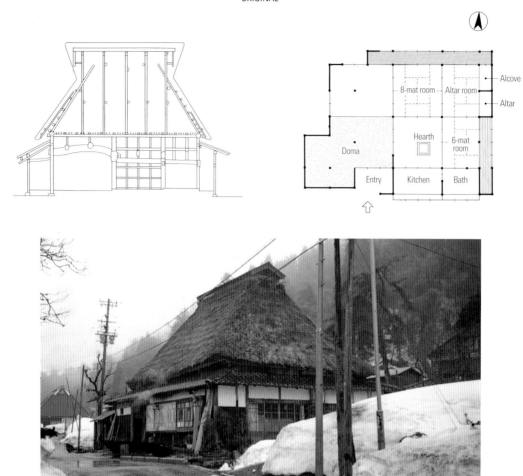

Alcove

8-mat room · Altar room

Altar

Doma · Hearth · 6-mat room

Entry · Kitchen · Bath

SECTION THROUGH—RENOVATED · MAIN FLOOR—RENOVATED

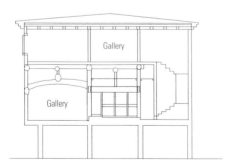

Gallery

Gallery

Office

DN · 4.5-mat room · Alcove

UP

6-mat room · Gallery

Fireplace

Entry

Taken from original 移築部分

ABOVE: A view of the original house in Ikeda-cho, Fukui Prefecture, in the 1980s.

RIGHT: The interlocking beams of the East Gallery are made of massive pine logs. The ceiling is white plaster.

上：福井県にあった移築する前の民家。右：一階天井の松材で作られた力強い梁組。

◀ PREVIOUS PAGE: The L-shaped living space of the East Gallery is unusual. Special wood flooring
has been used in order to accommodate underfloor heating.

前ページ：広間全景。床は床暖房が使えるフローリング。

ABOVE: The second floor of the East Gallery is devoted to a display of Imari porcelain.
LEFT: Large bowl, blue-and-white porcelain, Old Imari, mid-Edo period.

上：二階ギャラリー。古伊万里、竹花籠、額絵、漆器などのコレクションが展示してある。
下：蔵戸テーブルの上に置いた、染め付け古伊万里人物紋様大鉢（江戸中期）。

chapter 5

RENOVATED FOLK HOUSES

RIGHT: The approach to the Salomon Villa, located atop a mountain, shows how well the house fits in with the natural surroundings of the Karuizawa area. The location makes for an ideal vacation home.

軽井沢の自然に溶け込んだ外観。

THE SALOMON VILLA
A villa in the style of a farmhouse

The Salomons' vacation home, the first farmhouse I moved and reconstructed professionally, is situated in a 3,000-*tsubo* (about 9,900-square-meter/100,000-square-foot) grove cut from the top of a mountain, overlooking the Hanareyama mountains near Karuizawa. I have already related how it came to be built for Mrs. Salomon's birthday. Mrs. Salomon wanted to cultivate the land, so I selected a farmhouse from the upper reaches of the Kuzuryu River to be rebuilt as a farmhouse-style villa.

Mr. Salomon has a profound knowledge of architecture and has owned several beautiful homes, including the Azabu residence built by Antonin Raymond, a disciple of Frank Lloyd Wright. I carried out this first transfer under Mr. Salomon's guidance, and he taught me a great deal.

The construction of fireplaces, a simple kitchen, the wickerwork-pattern plasterwork under the roof, rush-mat floors, and so on—many details that I would later use often—are found here. I was led to think about the harmony of Western and Asian elements, and about comfortable living through the influence of Mr. Salomon. Sadly, Mrs. Salomon recently passed away, but Mr. Salomon is as fit as ever, and it is always a pleasure for me to have him look at my work.

サロモン邸
農家を移築した農家風の別荘

　私の移築民家第一号となったサロモン邸（別荘）は、軽井沢の離れ山を望む山の頂上を切り開いた3000坪の山林の中にある。夫人の誕生日のプレゼントとして建てられることになったいきさつは前にも述べた。この地で畑仕事をするのが夫人の希望だったので、九頭竜川上流域にあった農家を移築して農家風の別荘を計画した。

　サロモン氏は建築についての造詣が深く、ライトの弟子であるアントニー・レイモンドの建てた麻布のご自宅をはじめ、いくつかの美しい家をもっておられた。私にとって初の移築の仕事であるこのケースでは、氏の指示に従って建て、多くのことを教えられた。暖炉の作り方、シンプルな台所、屋根裏の網代漆喰、いぐさのマットなど、後々私の建築で多用することになった細部がすでにここにある。洋と和の調和やゆったりとした暮らし方を考えさせられたのも氏の影響だ。夫人は残念ながら一昨年亡くなられたが、サロモン氏は今もお元気で、彼にその後の仕事を見ていただくことを私は楽しみにしている。

MAIN FLOOR

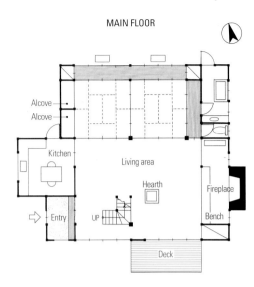

Alcove
Alcove
Kitchen
Living area
Hearth
Fireplace
Entry   UP   Bench
Deck

Taken from original　移築部分

SECOND FLOOR

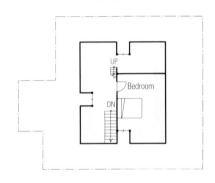

UP
Bedroom
DN

LOFT

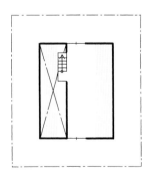

Seen in this view, the main living space remains almost unchanged from its original condition. The traditional *irori* hearth has been retained, as have the original floorboards. The view is handsomely framed by traditional sliding *shoji* doors.

居間。囲炉裏の上には太い縄でヒアマ（火天）が吊してある。床は旧民家の床材をそのまま使ってある。

CLOCKWISE, FROM TOP LEFT:

Rattan chairs suit the vacation ambiance of Karuizawa.

Mr. Solomon himself designed this fireplace, made from local stone. A comfortable built-in bench is nestled into the cozy sunken-floor area.

The loft bedroom features a style of window called *biraki-mado*.

FACING PAGE: The Japanese *irori* hearth meets the Western fireplace: a harmonious blend of cultures.

左上：居間の南にベランダが続き屋外の生活を楽しめる。藤の椅子を置いて。右上：一段低く作られたサロモン氏デザインの石製の暖炉。備え付けのベンチに座ってゆったりとくつろぐスペース。下：屋根裏部屋の開き窓。右：居間全景。

IRORI VERSUS FIREPLACES: Most people associate the *irori*, or sunken hearth, with *minka*. But a fireplace is simply more functional in daily life. Fireplaces are not only easier to build but safer. So, while I have built only five *irori* in my entire career, I have included fireplaces in every house. A firescreen makes it safe to leave the room with a fire burning, and a well-made fireplace does not fill the house with smoke. Often, a fire in the fireplace is less meaningful for the warmth it provides than for its beauty. In Hawaii, many people enjoy a fire in the fireplace while the air conditioner runs.

囲炉裏と暖炉：民家移築といえば、囲炉裏の雰囲気がイメージとして浮かぶのが当然であろう。しかし実生活においては暖炉のほうが有利である。囲炉裏は座って作業をするためにかなりの重労働である。また、灰が風で飛んだり、安全性のこともあるので私は5軒しか作っていない。一方暖炉は前にスクリーンを立てるため、留守にしても大丈夫であり、煙くもない。暖を取るというより目で楽しむものくらいに考えればよいと思う。ハワイの家では施主はエアコンをかけながら暖炉の火を楽しんでいた。

THE KARUIZAWA VILLA

A villa in the woods, with folk objects put to dramatic use

Situated in a quiet district of vacation homes in Kyu Karuizawa, this residence is also a reconstructed dwelling I transferred from the higher reaches of the Kuzuryu River.

At the time, the owner was the head of a large multinational business. Since overseas visitors were frequent, I built the villa to provide the comfort of Western-style living in a traditional Japanese dwelling. The home includes a large living room and fireplace, an overlooking tatami room on the mezzanine floor, and a bedroom beneath the *gassho* roof. The big veranda surrounding the west and south sides of the house was built in the image of the *soto niwa* garden used by farmers for drying their harvest. The outdoor-loving owners of the house use this area frequently. The barbecue corner I built on the veranda, to the rear of the fireplace, was particularly well received. When I am there, I feel like I can still hear the voices of the four children, who are now grown and doing great things abroad.

The inviting veranda above the southern slope of the site.

南斜面にはりだしたベランダ。

The owner's wife, while raised on the eastern coast of the United States, is very knowledgeable about Japanese culture, folk art, and Japanese interiors. She contributed her own bold ideas to the house, decorating the interior with everyday folk craft articles, such as the snow sled in the living room.

SIDE VIEW

軽井沢の別荘
民具を大胆に使った森の中の別荘

　旧軽井沢の静かな別荘地にあるK邸も、九頭竜川上流域から民家を移築した。当時氏は国際的な大企業の責任者で海外からの来客も多かったため、日本の民家に洋の暮らしやすさを意識して作った。大きなリビングや暖炉、それを見おろす中二階の和室、合掌屋根の下のベッドルームなどが美しく調和している。家の南西をとりまく大きなベランダは、収穫物の乾燥などの作業をする農家の外庭のイメージで作ったが、屋外の楽しみを知るこの家の人々にはよく利用された。とくに暖炉の外側に面して作ったバーベキューコーナーは好評だった。そこにいると、今では立派に成長して海外で活躍している4人の子供たちの声が、いつまでも聞こえているような気がする。

　アメリカ東海岸に育った夫人は、日本文化の教養が深く、民芸についての著書もある人だ。リビングに据えられた雪ぞりをはじめ、大胆に民具を使ったインテリアが工夫されている。

ORIGINAL

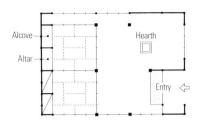

Alcove
Altar
Hearth
Entry →

A central feature of the living room is a hibachi-table made from a recycled zelkova beam.

欅のサシカモイ（差鴨居）で作った大きな火鉢兼テーブル。床はい草マットを敷き、床暖房を施してある。

The original house in Fukui Prefecture, in the 1980s.

移築する前の福井県の民家。

MAIN FLOOR

Alcove
Alcove
UP
DN
Kitchen/Dining
Bench
Living area
Entry →
Fireplace
Barbecue
Deck

MEZZANINE（中二階）

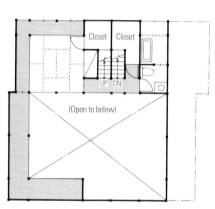

Closet
Closet
UP DN
(Open to below)

Taken from original　移築部分

SECOND FLOOR

Lounge
DN
UP
DN
Bedroom

LOFT

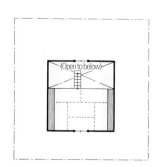

(Open to below)

The living room, flooded with light, has a sunny, inviting alcove at one end.

古民家特有の暗さと寒さを取り払い、明るく暖かく快適に作った居間。

ROOM ARRANGEMENT: Broadly speaking, *minka* interiors are of two types. One is high-ceilinged, usually associated with the earthen-floored *doma* and kitchen areas. The spaciousness of such interiors makes them suitable for large gatherings and for a lifestyle with chairs; they can be redesigned as large living-dining areas. Usually dark and cold in their original settings, they can be made more livable by enlarging apertures and adding heated floors. The second type of space is low-ceilinged, including the Buddhist altar room, sitting rooms, storeroom, veranda, and so on. Though the idea may offend some old-fashioned sensibilities, such spaces are best used for entryway halls, stairway halls, kitchens, bathrooms, and other areas connected to water. Also, the mezzanine usually found above the stable area (*umaya*) can be put to many uses. Most farmhouses have a decorative alcove (*tokonoma*) in the most formal sitting room. Even if this cannot be replicated exactly during remodeling, it is desirable to include it somewhere, albeit in an abbreviated form. Finally, the slanting *gassho* roof encloses a huge volume of space, so that a bedroom with attached bath, study, small living room, storage area, and so forth can all be fitted into the attic space. The best place to partition the attic is directly under the crossbeams.

間取り：民家の内部は大きく二つに分けられる。一つは天井の高い、ドマやダイドコ部分だ。広いのでたくさんの人が集う部屋や椅子の生活に適し、ダイニングを兼ねた大リビングに計画できる。ここは暗くて寒いところだったので、開口部を大きく取って明るくし、床暖房を入れて暖かくすると快適になる。二つめは天井の低い部分で、仏間、座敷、納戸、縁側などだ。昔の感覚では許されないことかもしれないが、玄関ホール、階段ホール、キッチン、浴室などの間取りに変更するのが機能的である。また、ウマヤの上にある中二階部分もいろいろな用途に使える。床の間はそのまま復元できない場合でもあきらめずに、どこかに移して略式にしてでも残したい。合掌屋根の下は広い。屋根裏部屋は浴室付き寝室、書庫、小さな居間、納戸などを計画できる。間仕切る場所は合掌材の真下がよい。

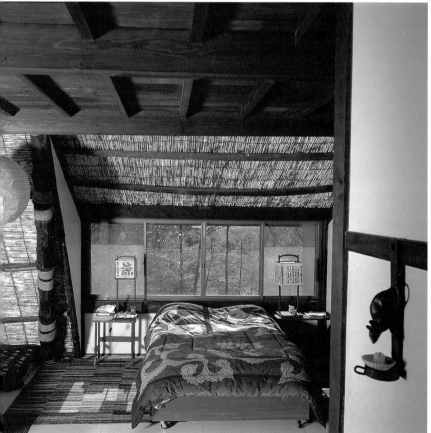

COUNTERCLOCKWISE, FROM TOP LEFT: The large Japanese room on the first floor features a round window which frames a view of Mount Asama.

The kitchen, with its built-in bench, wood table, and old tools on the wall, has a comfortable rustic flavor.

The fireplace is unusual in that it is set into a white plaster wall.

The bed in the second-floor bedroom is nestled into an intimate, slope-roofed nook.

The paper lantern by Isamu Noguchi accents the bedroom perfectly.

左上:一階八畳の和室。丸窓からは浅間山が見える。左下:キッチン東側のベンチ。下中:耐火煉瓦に漆喰を重ねて作った居間の暖炉。上:二階の寝室。イサムノグチの明かりが美しく調和している。下:二階寝室。低く押さえた天井が落ちついた雰囲気を作りだしている。

RIGHT: The entryway, visible here, leads to both the *gassho zukuri* wing and the *sukiya*-style wing.

玄関。右手の縁側廊下から数寄屋造りの建物につながる。

THE AMAKASU HOUSE

The *gassho*, reduced in size by half, is connected to a tea-ceremony–style cottage

The Amakasu House, located in a rural valley in Inamuragasaki, Kamakura, was built as a summer home in the style of a tea-ceremony pavilion in the early part of the Showa period (1926–89). The separate caretaker's house had become considerably dilapidated, and the difficulty of the assignment was in tearing that part down and adding a *gassho zukuri* dwelling to make a living room. Since the space was limited, I used only half of a little farmhouse from Imajo, in Fukui Prefecture. As if joining the tea-ceremony-style building to the *gassho zukuri* section without it seeming incongruous were not problem enough, the height of the former is only 2.8 meters (9 feet) to the ceiling, whereas the latter measures about 4 meters (13 feet). The difference in height caused great problems for connecting the second story. I cut a little from the base of the pillars in the *gassho zukuri* structure and reconciled the height difference in three stages. The staircase from the first floor turned or went up and down every few steps, creating four landings. The small window placed at each one of these now affords charming views of the valley.

When I was asked a few years later to build a library and a sauna as an extension to the same house, I made the exterior in the traditional *kura* (white-walled storehouse) style. With the original tea-ceremony–style pavilion in the middle, the three types of architecture blend well into the valley landscape.

The older tea-ceremony–style (*sukiya*) wing (left) of the Amakasu House is mated to a *gassho zukuri*–style wing (right).

夕暮れの甘糟邸全景。右側が合掌造り、左が数寄屋造りになっている。

ORIGINAL RENOVATED

甘糟邸
合掌を二分の一に縮小して数寄屋に連結

　鎌倉は稲村ヶ崎の谷戸の奥にある甘糟邸は、昭和の初めに夏の別荘として建てられた数寄屋造りの二階家だった。管理人室となっていた別棟の老朽化がひどく、その部分を取り壊して合掌造りの民家をつなげて居間を作るという難しい注文だった。まず面積の制限があったので福井県今庄で見つけた小ぶりな農家の半分だけを使うことにした。数寄屋に違和感なく合掌造りをつなげることも問題だったが、数寄屋の建物は天井までの高さが2m80cm、合掌造りは4mであり、二階をつなぐには高さの差がありすぎたことも大きな問題だった。合掌造りの柱の根元をすこし切り、三段の差をつけた。一階からの階段も数段ずつのぼったり曲ったり下りたりと踊り場を4ヵ所作ったが、その度に小さな窓から眺める谷戸の景色が変って楽しいものとなった。

　数年後に依頼された書庫とサウナの増築は、外観を蔵造りにした。数寄屋を挟んで合掌造り、蔵造りと三つの建築が谷戸の景色に溶け込んでいる。

MAIN FLOOR

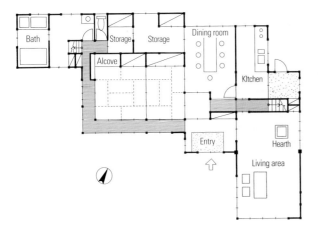

Taken from original　移築部分

MEZZANINE （中二階）

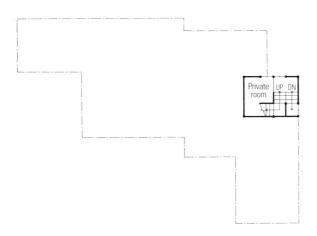

SECOND FLOOR

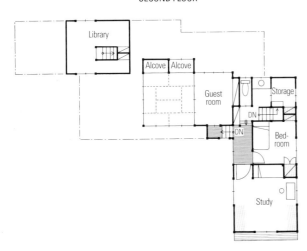

The heavy black beams of the main living space set off the delicacy of Taisho-period (1912–25) furniture.

一階居間。黒光りする太い梁と大正時代の家具が違和感なく
マッチして快適な空間を作っている。

LEFT TO RIGHT: This floor-level hearth is opened for use in winter and covered over in warmer months.

This stair landing receives light from a high window and is bordered by a large beam that is irresistibly inviting to the touch.

The bedroom and study on the second floor.

左：冬は囲炉裏を囲み、夏は蓋をしてフロアにできる。
上：四季の移り変わりを楽しめる階段踊り場。右：二階の寝室兼書斎。

RIGHT: The main living space of the Weber House. A Japanese room is visible beyond the sliding screens at the far end, while the entry, kitchen, and bath are concealed behind lacquered-wood sliding doors.

一階居間。正面は和室、右側の板戸を開けるとダイニングキッチン、バスルームなどの水回りがある。その上階は寝室とゲストルーム。

THE WEBER HOUSE

A pleasant interior just big enough for two

The Webers' vacation home, built near the sea at Hayama in Kanagawa Prefecture, was originally of simple construction. Mr. Weber, who is Swiss, told me that it was to be a house for spending relaxing weekends, and so a simple plan was best. Using a solid door, I divided the two 8-mat rooms adjoining the living room into a kitchen and utility room, and bath and toilet, making a compact arrangement. With the hipped roof in the form of *gassho* gables, I left the triangular area beneath the roof as it was: a large space, which could be used as a guest room or a game room, as desired. For the floor of the 33-mat-sized living room, I used the original boards from the house, which was brought from Fukui Prefecture. Mr. Weber greatly admired the beautiful, deep patina of these boards, used by earlier owners from the Edo period (1600–1868) on.

When Mr. Weber retired from working life ten years later, we added a second living room, bedroom, and bathroom for the couple in the area under the roof. Ten years after that, when they returned to Switzerland, real estate agents planned to demolish the house to make a vacant lot. Fortunately, the house was ultimately saved when someone who appreciates the value of *minka* bought it.

ウェーバー邸
築10年後の二人だけの快適空間

　神奈川県葉山の海近くに建てたウェーバー邸は、最初はシンプルな構造だった。スイス人のウェーバー氏は、週末をのんびり過ごす家だから簡単がいい、といわれたため、リビングに続く8畳間二つを板戸で仕切ってキッチンと家事室、浴室と手洗いをコンパクトに詰めた。寄棟を切妻合掌とした三角の屋根裏は大きな空間のまま残して、客室にもゲームルームにも自在に使えるようにした。33畳のリビングの床は、福井から移築した民家の板をそのまま使った。江戸時代から何代にもわたって、さまざまな人が踏みしめた床板の深い色調の良さを、ウェーバー氏は楽しんでくださった。

　建てて10年目に現役を退かれ、東京から葉山へ生活の拠点を移された時、屋根裏空間にご夫妻の居間、寝室、バスルームなどをあらためて作った。さらに10年、お二人がスイスに帰国される時、この家を壊して更地にする計画があったが、幸いに民家の価値を知る新オーナーに買いとられてことなきを得た。

Alcove

Entry

Kitchen

Living area

Fireplace

Taken from original　移築部分

ABOVE: The kitchen, framed by the sliding doors.

RIGHT: A view from above. The Weber House retains its original pine flooring.

上：簡素なダイニングキッチン。右：中二階から見た居間。床材はオリジナルの松板を使っている。

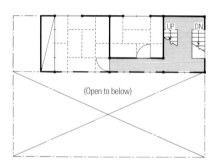

MEZZANINE（中二階）

UP　DN

(Open to below)

SLIDING DOORS: Old *minka* contain surprisingly few doors that can be salvaged for reuse. Paneled doors that have been polished by hand for generations are impressive. They should be used as partitions in large rooms with strong columns and rafters, even if they must be repaired. Removable sliding doors, including sliding panels covered with heavy paper (*fusuma*) and translucent sliding screens (*shoji*), make it easy to freely convert smaller rooms into one large one. Sliding doors did not provide much privacy or security in the past, but recently new kinds of locks have been developed that largely solve the security problem.

As rooms with solid walls grow more common, the reuse of *fusuma*, *shoji*, and transoms (*ranma*) as primary spatial dividers has decreased. *Shoji*, however, are invaluable as a way of letting in light, and the thin sheet of handmade *washi* paper with which they are covered provides surprisingly good heat insulation. Combining *shoji* with curtains or hangings in a bedroom makes it possible to vary the decor by day and night. For outdoor fittings—particularly storm doors (*amado*)—new aluminum items are preferable to the traditional wood for their superior soundproofing, security, and ease of upkeep.

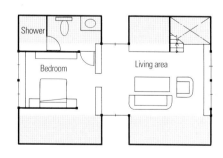

SECOND FLOOR

Shower

Bedroom

Living area

建具：民家移築のとき、再利用できる建具は意外と少ない。長年磨きあげられた板戸は、重厚感があるので、力強い柱や梁のある大部屋を間仕切るのに最適である。修理してでもぜひ利用したい。この板戸を含め、襖や障子などの引き戸は、簡単に取り外せるので、間仕切りを取れば二つの部屋が一つになり開放感が得られるという、日本独自の貴重な建具である。板戸のような引き戸は、プライバシーを必要とする部屋には向いていなかったが、近年上等な施錠が開発され、ロックが容易になっている。壁で囲う個室が増えて、間仕切りとしての襖、障子、欄間などの再利用が少なくなった。しかし、明かり取りとしての障子は欠かせない存在だ。和紙一重とはいえ、かなりの断熱効果がある。寝室でもカーテンもしくは幕と併用すれば、昼夜、異なるインテリアが楽しめる。なお外回りの建具は、木製をやめてアルミのサッシに決めている。防音、断熱効果、施錠、維持管理で有利だと思う。

LEFT: An additional shower and toilet are located on the second floor.

RIGHT AND BELOW: At the time of the original reconstruction, the second floor was left as a large unfurnished space (right). Ten years later (below) it was completed as a second living room.

左：移築10年後に作った二階トイレ。奥にシャワーがある。下：二階屋根裏。セカンド・リビングルームになっている。右：移築当時の二階屋根裏。ゲストルームや予備の部屋としてとして使われた。合掌梁がよく見える。

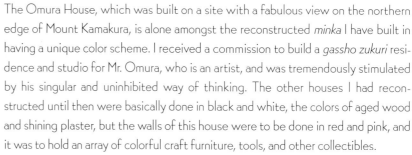

RIGHT: Details, such as this chandelier over the dining table, are the product of the owner's unique creative sensibility.

サンルームへとつながるダイニングコーナー。テーブルの真上にはシャンデリアが輝く。

THE OMURA HOUSE & STUDIO
A bright-red spiral staircase and a colorful interior

Color is a byword at the Omura House. A bright-red spiral staircase springs up from the entryway.

玄関ホールの吹抜に建つ赤い螺旋階段。

The Omura House, which was built on a site with a fabulous view on the northern edge of Mount Kamakura, is alone amongst the reconstructed *minka* I have built in having a unique color scheme. I received a commission to build a *gassho zukuri* residence and studio for Mr. Omura, who is an artist, and was tremendously stimulated by his singular and uninhibited way of thinking. The other houses I had reconstructed until then were basically done in black and white, the colors of aged wood and shining plaster, but the walls of this house were to be done in red and pink, and it was to hold an array of colorful craft furniture, tools, and other collectibles.

On entering, one is immediately struck by the bright-red iron spiral staircase that rises to the ceiling. Climbing this staircase leads to a studio under the roof. I kept the slope of the roof gentle to make a gabled second story, letting in natural light by opening a large glass-window section to the south. For the first-floor living room, I used many large windows, and substituted curtains in the various colors chosen by Mr. Omura for sliding *shoji* doors. Textile wall hangings and curtains in various colors are draped throughout the house. The fact that this space, where there is both a sunken *irori* hearth and a normal fireplace, is so much fun and yet so relaxing, is surely due to the fact that Mr. Omura's sensibility provides a strong sense of unity. I affectionately call this house the *toki yakata*, the "crested ibis house," a play on the word *toki iro*, "crested ibis color," which refers to the shade of pale pink of this bird.

大村邸
カラフルなインテリアに真っ赤な螺旋階段

　鎌倉山の北の端に建つ眺望絶景の大村邸は、私の建てた移築民家の中で一つだけ独特の色彩をもっている。大村氏は画家で、アトリエと住居を合掌民家で、と依頼された。自由でユニークな発想にはおおいに刺激を受けた。それまでの移築民家は黒と白が基調だったが、この家の壁は赤やピンク、調度品や蒐集品もカラフルな民芸品が多い。何より玄関を入ってまず目に入るのは、天井までの吹き抜けの空間に伸びる真っ赤に塗られた鉄骨製の螺旋階段である。この赤い階段をのぼると屋根裏部分にアトリエがある。屋根の勾配をゆるくとって切妻総二階とし、南に大きなガラスの開口部を設け自然光をとり入れた。一階のリビングにも開放的な大きな窓を多用し、障子を使わず大村氏の選んだ色とりどりのカーテンを使った。さまざまな色の布が下がり、敷かれている。暖炉と囲炉裏が同居しているこの空間が楽しさと落着きをもっているのは、大村氏の感覚が強いイメージの統一感をもっているからだろう。私はこの家を愛着を込めて「トキ館（ヤカタ）」とよんでいる。

MAIN FLOOR

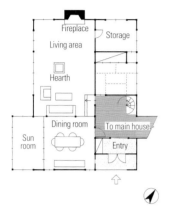

Fireplace
Living area
Storage
Hearth
Sun room
Dining room
To main house
Entry

Taken from original 移築部分

MEZZANINE（中二階）

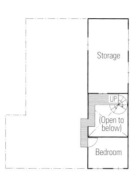

Storage
UP
(Open to below)
Bedroom

SECOND FLOOR

Studio
Bedroom
Bath

LOFT

(Open to below)

A lively combination of rugs and cushions sur-
rounds the traditional *irori* hearth.

居間からスキップして続くダイニングを見通す。

CLOCKWISE, FROM LEFT: The atelier on the second floor, with the light of the guest room visible through the windows above. The narrow stair is the owner's original design, based on Southeast Asian examples.

Posters and artwork fill the atelier space.

A collection of antiques seems right at home with one of the owner's paintings.

左：二階のアトリエ。こちらも壁はピンクに。三階のゲストルームに上がる梯子は大村氏デザイン。
上：アトリエに飾られた作品。下：アンティックの人形や時計のコレクション。

RIGHT: "Flow-through" space is a hallmark of Japanese architecture, and here the vista runs from the entryway in the foreground all the way to the woods beyond.

玄関。入りやすい低めの上がり框。

THE TAGAWA VILLA
A *gassho zukuri* dream house with pillars dating back to 1807

The Tagawas, who run a trading company and have lived abroad, often entertain guests from overseas. In response to their desire to build a second home that shows the traditional Japanese way of life, I chose a two-hundred-year-old *minka* from Gifu Prefecture.

The home site is located in a hot springs village with lots of vacation homes. The Minami Hakone Golf Course spreads away to the south, and a view of Mount Fuji to the west. Making a hipped roof with *gassho* gables, I set the entrance under the eaves so that one enters the house directly from the golf course. The golf-loving couple have a glorious view of the course from the second-floor bedroom, and Mount Fuji towers over the guest room on the opposite side.

The main pillar in the center of the spacious living room on the first floor is unusual in having the date of construction (1804) carved into it. In keeping with the period, antique folk articles have been arranged to re-create old Japan. For Mrs. Tagawa, who is very fond of cooking, I included a commercial range, and an oven with a ventilator fan. The bath uses hot-spring water and is made from *izuishi* stone, the color of which turns a stunning pale green when the bath is filled.

The southern façade of the Tagawa Villa presents a neat, well-proportioned appearance.

外観南面。

田川邸
大黒柱に記された文化四年の刻印

　貿易会社を経営し、外国暮らしの経験もある田川夫妻には海外からの来客も多い。「これが日本の住まいだ」と誇れるようなセカンドハウスを建てたい、という希望に応えて、築200年の岐阜の民家を選んだ。

　場所は南箱根のゴルフコースが南に広がり、西に富士山を望む温泉付別荘地だった。寄棟を切妻合掌としてゴルフ場からまっすぐにこの家に入る形で、玄関を妻入りにした。ゴルフ好きのご夫妻の二階の寝室からはゴルフコースが一望でき、反対側の客室の正面には富士山がそびえている。

　一階の広々したリビングの中央にある大黒柱に、文化四年（1807年）と建てた年が刻まれているのも珍しかったが、その年代にふさわしい古民具を配して、古き良き日本を再現した。

　厨房には料理好きの夫人のために業務用コンロ、オーブンに業務用の換気設備をつけた。温泉の浴室には伊豆石を使っている。湯を張ったときの石が薄緑になり美しい。

MAIN FLOOR   MEZZANINE（中二階）

Deck

Fireplace

Living area

Dining area

Alcove   Entry   Kitchen

Taken from original　移築部分

(Open to below)

Alcove

Alcove

UP
DN

Storage

Alcove Alcove

SECOND FLOOR

Storage

Guest room

Bedroom

Shower

The main living space is well illuminated by
traditional sliding *shoji* doors as well as by a floor
lantern and a fireplace.

一階居間。障子は光をやさしく取り込み、熱を逃がさ
ない優れた建具である。開け放して充分な通風を得
ることもできる。

CLOCKWISE, FROM LEFT: Expansive but intimate, the Tagawa House living-dining room is strongly framed by zelkova columns and pine beams. Behind the lacquered sliding doors is a low-ceilinged Japanese room. The wheeled chest on the right conceals a bar (see photo below) and an entire audio-visual system.

The fully modern kitchen benefits from its high sloping ceiling.

A small triangular window adorns the bedroom.

左：一階ダイニングコーナー。吹抜けの高い天井を横切る松の梁、欅の柱が、安定感あふれる力強い空間を作る。右上：広いキッチンには業務用のオーブンレンジ、食器洗い機など、すべての機能が備わっている。下：車箪笥の中にはオーディオとバーが収納されている。右下：二階寝室。三角形の妻飾りから明かりを取る。

KITCHENS: Many original elements of traditional *minka* can and should be retained, but the dirt-floored kitchen is definitely not one of them. Not only does the homemaker spend a lot of time here, but the incorporation of a dining area usually makes the kitchen a center of family life, deserving great attention. Modern "system" kitchens—convenient and easy to clean—should be used if possible, in addition to a large window over the sink to let in light and offer a view of the outdoors. Work space, storage space, and utilities should be close at hand for ease in preparing food. Locating the kitchen near the large living room makes hosting parties easy.

台所：時代が変わっても、変えて良いものと変えてはいけないものがある。民家のダイドコはぜひ変えたい。主婦がいちばん長くいるところであるうえに、ダイニングキッチンにすれば家族が集うところになる。この場所は間取りのなかで最優先させたい。できればシステムキッチンにして、合理的で清潔に、流しの前面に自然を取り込む大きな窓を設けて明るく、食品庫とユーティリティを隣接させて便利に、そして大きなリビングを近接させてホームパーティーも楽々できるように計画したい。

RIGHT: The heavy grid of black structural elements and white plaster, combined with warm, golden-hued flooring, gives this living space a remarkable character.

白い漆喰に黒い格子の一階居間。囲炉裏の和室と奥の和室 (床の間) が見える。

THE AKIYAMA HOUSE

Originally the *gassho zukuri* farmhouse of a wealthy farmer; now a spacious 45-mat living area

This family home is situated in a residential area in the vicinity of Zushi Station in Kanagawa Prefecture. Mr. and Mrs. Akiyama and their two children visited my home, and having apparently been very impressed, canceled the design contract they had already drawn up with another builder and requested a reconstructed *minka*. Since they entrusted me with the interior design as well, I was able to make everything just as I imagined, right down to the smallest details.

I brought the original dwelling—a large, T-shaped building belonging to a wealthy farmer—from Fukui, planning a four-story *gassho zukuri* house with all modern conveniences. The ceiling of the first floor is 4 meters (13 feet) high. The short, soot-blackened supporting pillars and beams intersect in a grid pattern on the surface of the walls of the 45-mat living room, creating a dynamic design against the white walls. This is not simply a design, but an important feature in supporting the weight of the building and preventing lateral movement.

I used new materials in the children's room on the second floor, making it a lighter and brighter space. In the dressing room on the second floor, I installed a laundry chute leading to the washing machine a floor below. This traditional *minka* now has a German-style kitchen and a bath on the second floor with a Jacuzzi. Finally, I built a three-car garage in front of the large gate.

秋山邸
45畳のリビング、元豪農の合掌造り

　神奈川県の逗子駅近くの住宅地にある秋山邸は、会社を経営するご主人とふたりの子供を含む4人家族の日常の住居である。ご夫妻で私の家を訪ねて来られたが、強い印象を受けたようで、既に建築計画を立てて契約まで結ばれていたメーカーをキャンセルして移築民家を希望された。インテリアまで一任されたので、細部までイメージどおりに作ることができた。

　快適な最新機能を備えた四層の合掌造りの住宅を計画して福井より移築した民家は、T字型の大型な豪農の建物だった。一階の天井までの高さも4mを超えている。45畳のリビングの壁面は、煤で黒くなったツカとヌキが交差して白壁に格子模様を描き出し、ダイナミックな意匠を作りだしている。これは意匠だけでなく、建物の重さを支え横揺れを防ぐ大切な部分だ。

　二階の子供室は新材を使って明るい部屋にし、二階の脱衣室からは洗濯物を入れると一階の洗濯機まで筒状のパイプシャフトで届くシュートを設けた。厨房はドイツ製のシステムキッチンを、二階の浴室にはジャグジーバスを民家の空間に納めた。また、車3台の駐車場を大きな門の正面に設けた。

RENOVATED—SECTION THROUGH

3rd Floor
2nd Floor
Mezzanine
（中二階）

MAIN FLOOR

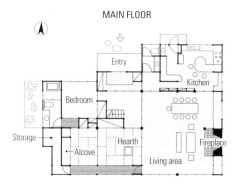

Entry
Kitchen
Bedroom
Storage
Hearth
Fireplace
Alcove
Living area

Taken from original　移築部分

MEZZANINE（中二階）

Bar
Lounge
Storage
UP
DN
UP
(Open to below)
Alcove
(Open to below)

SECOND FLOOR

Closet
DN
Children's room
DN
UP
Study
UP
Bedroom

THIRD FLOOR

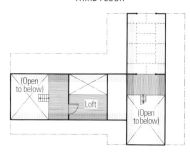

(Open to below)
Loft
(Open to below)

ORIGINAL

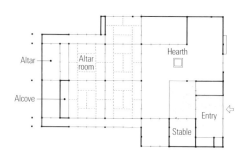

Altar
Altar room
Hearth
Alcove
Entry
Stable

CLOCKWISE, FROM BELOW: The entryway is a striking composition of straight and curved lines, and has a beautiful step-up platform. Light seems to filter in from an invisible source. ■ The natural green light of the lawn outside enhances the dark tones of the interior. ■ The seating area, set off by furniture and an antique chest, seems to focus on both the fireplace and the strikingly placed ink painting above it.

下：屏風が置かれた式台付きの玄関。右上：中二階から見おろす居間。広く取った開放部から自然を十分に取り込む。右下：時代箪笥をサイドテーブルに使った、暖炉の前のくつろぎのスペース。飾られた絵は雲谷等益筆の猿猴の図（1640年）。

ENTRYWAYS: The entryway of a house is its face, and in many respects it is the face of the owner as well. As such, its design is crucial. The ultimate location of the entryway in a renovated house should not be constrained by its original location nor by southern exposure; instead, a practical decision should be made based on the new environment and conditions. Great freedom is possible, such as converting a small tatami sitting room into a new entryway. Using a Western-style hinged door (generally more secure and more airtight than a sliding door) and lowering the size of the step up from the area where shoes are removed makes coming and going easy and convenient. But if a little inconvenience is not an issue, there is nothing to prevent the use of a sliding door and a high step in cases where the owner wants to keep more of the old-fashioned atmosphere.

玄関：玄関は家の顔といわれるほど大切な部分である。その位置を決めるには、元の場所とか南向きにこだわらず、移築する土地の環境や条件を合理的に判断するべきである。自由な発想で、座敷の一つを新しい玄関に計画することも可能である。一般的には「引き戸」よりも施錠と気密性に優れている「ドア」を玄関戸にして、靴を脱いで上がるときの段差を小さくすれば、出入りが楽で合理的だろう。一方、多少の不便を覚悟で、格式のある昔風の雰囲気を重んずるのであれば、引き戸にして上がり框を高くする玄関も考えられる。

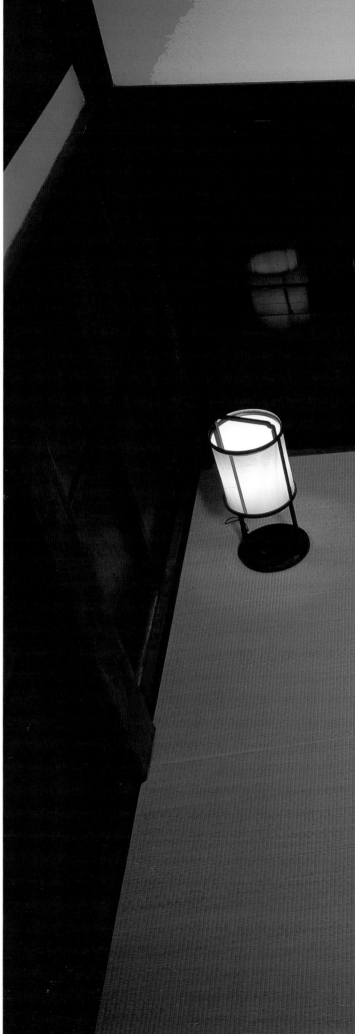

ABOVE: This multipurpose room, ideal for guests, opens onto an enclosed veranda with a view of the garden.

RIGHT: Bathed in gentle light and shadow, this tatami-matted room is made for human communication. The tatami themselves can be used very flexibly for sitting or reclining, and are easy to clean.

上：一階和室六畳。縁側から瀟洒な庭につながる。右：一階の囲炉裏を切った八畳間。畳の部屋は接客、寝室、客室などと多目的に使えるので便利だ。

LANTERNS: In the old days, lanterns used camellia oil and wicks, or candles. Today, they can be wired and fitted with incandescent bulbs for a pleasing effect, allowing the light, softened by handmade *washi* paper, to wash over the surrounding area. Lanterns are an indispensable atmospheric lighting element for remodeled *minka*.

行灯：行灯は昔、椿油やろうそくを燃やした。今は電気配線して白熱球を使えば、和紙を通してやさしい光があたりを包み、民家移築の空間には欠かせない貴重な人工照明器具である。

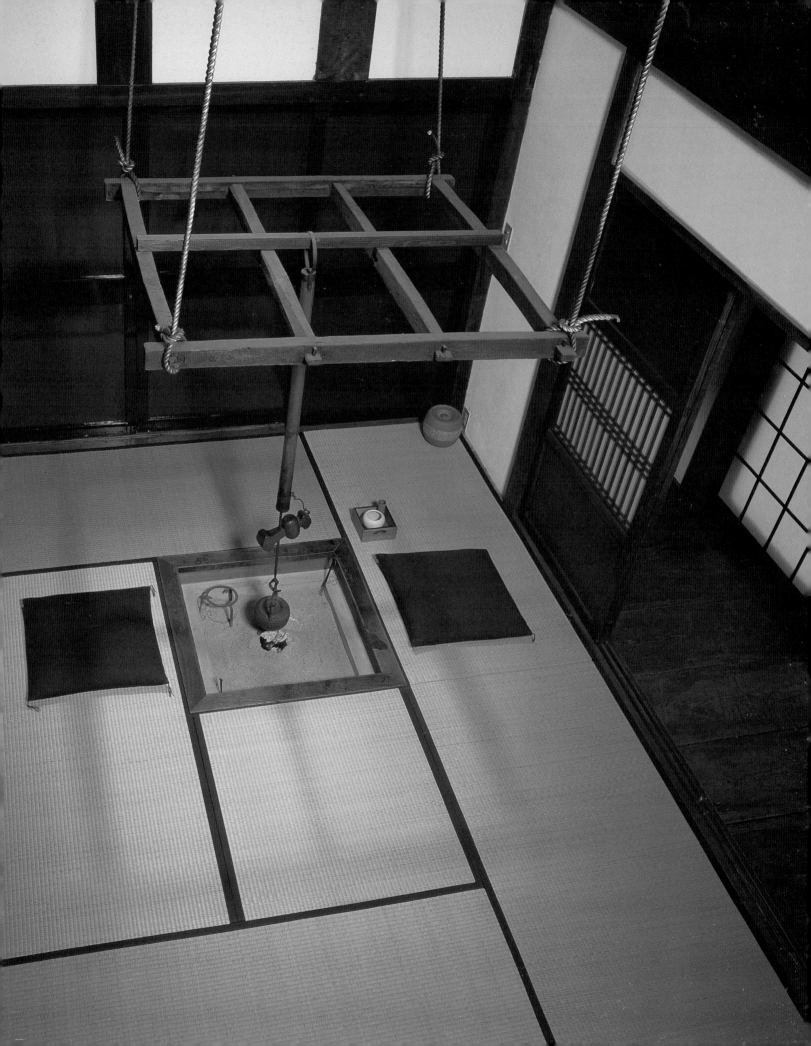

COUNTERCLOCKWISE, FROM RIGHT: The mezzanine floor. The golden column is actually a gold-leafed laundry chute.

The laundry chute frames one end of the bar.

The view up the stairs from the mezzanine to the second floor.

上：中二階のラウンジ、バーカウンター手前の黄金の丸柱は洗濯物を落とすためのシュート。左下：中二階のバー。仲間が集うスペース。右下：中二階踊り場から二階を見上げる。

ABOVE: The rich texture of the ceiling treatment and the rope-wrapped roof timbers lend the second-floor bedroom a strong handmade character.

LEFT: An intimate extra room is fitted into the triangular attic space.

上：二階の主寝室。下：三階屋根裏の和室。

RIGHT: This exterior view shows how the lower roof line of the house makes it less obtrusive amid the surrounding greenery.

屋根勾配をゆるやかにした外観。

THE KORVER HOUSE

The slope of the *gassho zukuri*–style roof has been adapted to conform to height restrictions

The entryway of the Korver House makes use of traditional sliding *shoji* doors, with the conventional Japanese paper being replaced by white glass.

玄関。ガラスの引き違い戸を使っている。

The Hiroyama area of Zushi has a large minimum lot size of 300 *tsubo* (990 square meters/10,600 square feet) and boasts an array of large, beautiful homes. Not only are telegraph poles kept out of sight, but it is rumored that the residents' association even vetoes plans for building designs they consider potential eyesores. Mr. Korver, a missionary and university lecturer, and his wife came to me with the request for a simple residence with the warm feel of wood. In accordance with the height limitation for building agreed on by the residents, a high-roofed *gassho zukuri* structure would not have been allowed, so I made a gently sloping roof.

In the southeastern section of the first floor, I made a room, with bath and toilet attached, for Mrs. Korver's 84-year-old mother. *Kamakurabori* (carved lacquerware) fittings decorated with plum, pine, and bamboo motifs, made by hand by the mother herself, were used in several places in the house. Mrs. Korver's mother is a Japanese woman who married a former German prisoner of war, one of the legendary group that was the first to perform Beethoven's Ninth Symphony in Japan.

I installed long boards for a bay window in the living room, arranging cushions over the boards so they could double as a bench. The end result was a restrained and tasteful residence.

コーバー邸
高さ制限で勾配をゆるやかにした合掌造り

　逗子の披露山は一区画が最低300坪と広く、美しい大きな邸宅が連なっている。電柱が見えないだけでなく、醜い建物は住民の会に拒否される、という噂もあるほどだ。宣教師で大学教授でもあるコーバー氏と夫人は、この住宅地にシンプルで木のぬくもりのある住まいを建てたいと希望された。

　住民の建築協定にある高さ制限からいって、高い屋根をもつ合掌造りは無理だったので、屋根の勾配をゆるやかにした。

　一階の南東の位置にまずコーバー夫人の84歳になる母上のために、浴室、トイレに隣接して部屋を作った。母上お手製の松竹梅を配した鎌倉彫の建具を数ヵ所にはめ込んだ。母上は日本で初めてベートーベンの第九を演奏した伝説のドイツ人捕虜の一人バート氏と結婚した日本女性である。

　リビングの窓際には出窓風に長いカウンターのような板を張り、座蒲団を並べたベンチとした。全体に趣味性の高い、親しみやすくおだやかな住居となった。

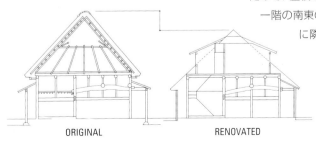

ORIGINAL　　　　RENOVATED

MAIN FLOOR

Taken from original 移築部分

SECOND FLOOR

The living-dining area. Natural wood floors are used, and a collection of antique bronzes graces the fireplace mantel. What appear to be small high-placed windows are actually speaker enclosures.

暖炉の前のくつろぎコーナーと、庭に面したダイニングコーナーで構成された一階居間。床は天然木を使っている。

LEFT: The deck affords an excellent view of the Zushi oceanside.

BELOW: The Korver House family room. The kitchen is located behind the carved wooden hutch.

上：ベランダからは逗子の海が見渡せる。下：ファミリールームの丸テーブル。鎌倉彫の食器棚（ハッチ）の向こうはキッチン。

TOP: The kitchen is high ceilinged, with windows to let in ample light.

BOTTOM: The view downstairs from the second floor. A matted alcove is used for display, as are the beams themselves.

上：窓をふんだんにとって明るく作ったキッチン。下：階段の踊り場に作られた飾り床。

STAIRS: In *gassho zukuri minka*, since the second floor and above were not living spaces, a single ladder sufficed for access to the upper reaches of the house. Consequently, remodeled *minka* need stairs, and their design is an especially rewarding opportunity. Providing sufficient headroom is always a challenge and usually requires converting a downstairs room into a stair well, with a landing at the mezzanine level. Originally intended for storage, the mezzanine is a place where the high beams and rafters can be physically touched. It makes a fine gallery for the display of collections, easily visible when ascending or descending the stairs. Although the distance to the second floor is not great, since the top of the stairs, located under the steep roof, will tend to be dark, care must be taken to provide a source of natural light.

階段：合掌民家の二階以上には人は住まなかったので、二階まで届く長い梯子が1本あれば用は足り、階段は必要とされなかった。そのため、民家移築では階段の計画はもっともやりがいのある仕事の一つで、一種の見せ場でもある。たくさんの梁に頭をぶつけないように、しかもゆったりとのぼれるようにする。そのためには座敷を一つ階段ホールとして使う覚悟がいる。中二階のレベルで踊り場を作るのが良い。中二階は物置に使用されたところだが、民家の構造材である桁や梁などに手が触れられる位置である。踊り場周辺に好みのコレクションを飾れば、のぼりおりの度に目を楽しませてくれるギャラリーになる。ここから二階はすぐだが、上がった所は合掌屋根の下で暗いので、外の光をうまく取り入れる工夫が必要だ。

RIGHT: The entryway makes extensive use of zelkova wood, such as in the stepping-up platform. The result is a very classic Japanese feeling.

欅の式台を配した玄関。正面に箪笥を置き、しつらえて客を迎える。

THE HAYASHI HOUSE

A relaxed effect gained by covering the floor with cork

Mr. Hayashi, owner-chef of a Tokyo restaurant, asked me to build him a second house in a village in the mountains near Kanagawa Prefecture's Lake Sagami. I was surprised to learn from an elderly inhabitant of the area that it had formerly been an underpopulated village dubbed "the Tibet of Kanagawa." The low residential density also meant that the plot was substantial. I was able to carry out a large-scale plan, including outbuildings and other structures, from the imposing gate to the fences and barnlike garage, all highlighting the best features of the former house to good advantage.

I laid thin cork flooring and put in subfloor heating in the big first-floor living room, dividing it into a place for sitting around the sunken hearth and an area with chairs in front of the fireplace. I made plenty of spaces for relaxing and for play. For example, the area at the eastern end of the house, reached by a connecting corridor, has a sunroom to the south and a game room (bar and mah-jongg room) to the north, centered on a large bathroom. Outside along the eastern exposure I built an airy, glass-enclosed area containing a Jacuzzi and a corner for practicing golf. On the second floor there is a billiards room, and still further up on the top floor is a lounge.

The Japanese-style room next to the south-facing entrance was Mr. Hayashi's mother's room. I still cannot forget the sight of Mr. Hayashi carrying his mother, piggyback style, into the room when it was completed.

One of the most attractive aspects of a *gassho zukuri* house is its tall, protective roof, as seen here in the Hayashi House. Windows can be added to the upper floors through the use of recesses, as in this case, or by adding baylike projections.

外観。屋根に作った入り窓がアクセント。

林邸
リビングに薄いコルク材を敷いたくつろぎの空間

　東京のオーナーシェフである林氏にセカンドハウスをと依頼された場所は、神奈川県は相模湖近くの山村だった。土地の古老に、ここは神奈川のチベット、過疎の村などといわれて驚いたが、それだけに広々とした敷地だった。門構えから塀、納屋風の大ガレージなどの附属物まで、思いどおりの大きな構想で古民家の良さを活かすことができた。

　一階の広いリビングの床は薄いコルク材を敷いた床暖房にし、囲炉裏を囲んで座る場所と暖炉の前の椅子のスペースに分けた。くつろぐ場所、遊びの場所を随所に設け、たとえば渡り廊下の行き着く東端に、湯殿を中心に南にサンルーム、北にゲームルーム（バー、マージャン室）、東の屋外にジャグジーバスとゴルフの練習コーナーを隣接させて、開放的なガラス張りとした。二階にビリヤード、さらにのぼって屋根裏にラウンジがある。

　南に面した玄関に続く和室をご母堂の部屋としたが、完成時、母上を背負ってこの部屋に入った林氏の姿は今も忘れられない。

MAIN FLOOR

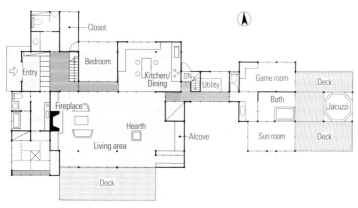

Closet

Entry

Bedroom

Kitchen/Dining

DN

Utility

Game room

Deck

Bath

Jacuzzi

Fireplace

Hearth

Alcove

Sun room

Deck

Living area

Deck

Taken from original 移築部分

ORIGINAL

Alcove

Altar

Altar room

Dei

Alcove

Toilet

Hearth

Entry

Daidoko (Kitchen)

Bath

Toilet

MEZZANINE（中二階）

UP — DN

(Open to below)

BELOW: The living room seen from the small mezzanine openings.

RIGHT: An unusual cork flooring accommodates subfloor heating. The kitchen is visible at the rear.

下：中二階和室の小窓から一階居間を見る。右：古風な囲炉裏がしゃれた居間にうまく調和している。床材はコルクを使って床暖房を施してある。

SECOND FLOOR

DN

Billiards room

Bedroom

UP

LOFT

(Open to below)

LEFT: The inviting warmth of the house is evident in this evening shot of the exterior.

ABOVE: The stairway of the Hayashi House ascends directly from the entrance hall, visible here from the living room.

左：庭からベランダごしに居間を見る。上：一階玄関ホールに作った階段。

ABOVE: The Hayashi House possesses an enviable combination of relaxing features. A Jacuzzi is located outside the glassed-in traditional bath, which also leads to a game room (to the left) and a sun room (to the right). A golf putting area lies outside, next to the Jacuzzi.

RIGHT: The waist-high partitions, which afford some privacy for the toilet area, are not an original feature, but harmonize well with the rest of the interior.

上：快適な湯殿。奥にジャグジー、左側はゲームルーム、右側はサンルームと大人の楽園のようだ。下：一階玄関北側のトイレ。ゆったりと作ってある。

ABOVE: The billiards room on the second floor.

LEFT: The third-floor attic space has been converted into an intimate lounge room.

上：二階のビリヤードルーム。下：三階屋根裏のラウンジ。

RIGHT: A view of the guest rooms across the central corridor. In order to give foreign guests a taste of the Japanese lifestyle, beds are absent and futon are laid out at night.

和室の素晴らしさを意識して設計した。

THE UNION BANK OF SWITZERLAND GUESTHOUSE

An open-air bath comprises the essence of Japanese bathing culture

Mr. Linderknecht, an executive of the Union Bank of Switzerland, visited my house, and soon after I received a commission for a guesthouse to be made from a similar *minka*. The building site was on the banks of Lake Yamanaka in a national park, so I thought about how to work without altering the surrounding environment. Using a sloping piece of land, I set a large garage half underground, adjoining the boiler room, thus keeping the noise and smell at a distance. So that rainwater would seep naturally into the plot, I dug a deep well-like hole. I also made a separate structure containing a large bathhouse with a filtration apparatus. Enclosing it in glass on every side to give the feeling of an outdoor bath, I laid *izuishi* stone for the overflows and on the bottom of the plain cypress wood rim of the bathtub, encouraging a very Japanese sense of the outdoor-bath experience. The corridor linking the bathhouse to the main building has glass doors on each side, reinforcing the sensation that one is outdoors. The living and dining rooms of the main building also serve as meeting rooms.

Once building began, a Swiss architect came to Japan to oversee the site, and taking a great interest in Japanese *minka* architecture, he insured that the project was beautifully realized.

The exterior showing the main house (right) and the connected bathhouse (left).

外観。廊下でつながる左手の低い建物は湯殿。

スイス・ユニオン銀行ゲストハウス
日本の入浴文化を凝縮した露天風の湯殿

　スイス銀行の重役リンダークネヒト氏が私の家に寄られて間もなく、同じような民家でゲストハウスを、と依頼された。建築の場所は山中湖畔で国立公園の中だったので、周囲の環境を変えぬよう工夫した。斜面の敷地を利用して、大ガレージを半地下とし、ボイラー室をこれに隣接させて音と匂いを遠ざけた。雨水は敷地間に自然に浸透するよう井戸のような深い穴を掘った。また、濾過装置をつけた大きな湯殿を別棟に作り露天風呂の雰囲気をだして総ガラス張りにし、壁面には檜の白木を、浴槽と洗い場には伊豆石を用い、リラックスを楽しむ日本の入浴文化を示した。浴室から本館につながる渡り廊下は両側をガラス戸にして、屋外を歩いているような雰囲気をもたせている。本館のリビングルームとダイニングルームは会議室も兼ねている。

　工事が始まるとスイスから建築家が来日して現場の監督をつとめたが、日本の民家建築に興味をもって見守ってくれた。

MAIN FLOOR

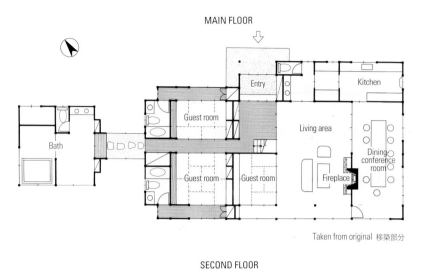

Taken from original 移築部分

SECOND FLOOR

SECTION THROUGH

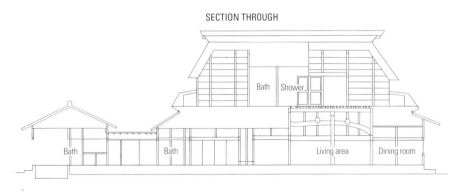

RIGHT: The natural darkness of the interior is mitigated by large openings, while a strong pair of beams intersect a third beam, which is acutely arched. The underside of these large beams reflects light in a rich and beautiful way.

一階居間。カーブした力強い梁がアクセント。

APERTURES AND VENTILATION: When rebuilding a *minka* in a new location, it is advisable to study the light and wind conditions of the new site and rethink the room layout entirely with them in mind. The subtropical Japanese climate, with its frequent rain and hot, humid summers, makes large apertures essential throughout the house. They will ensure good ventilation, provide views of the outdoors and admit fresh breezes. Old *minka* have surprisingly few solid walls, and with lattice doors, transom windows, and paper-covered sliding *shoji* doors that let in the light, they are well adapted to the Japanese climate. Sunlight filtered through *shoji* provides the finest possible natural lighting for Japanese houses, another reason sliding doors should be used extensively.

開口部と通風：民家移築では、新しい土地の光と風をよく理解して、白紙の状態で間取りを考えるのがよい。日本の風土は夏は高温多湿で雨が多く蒸し暑いので、開口部をなるべく大きくしかもあちこちに作り、通風の良さを確保したいし、自然の眺めや風を屋内に取り込みたい。古民家は驚くほど壁が少なく、まさしく日本の風土に適した建築である。こうした貴重な開口部に格子戸とか明かり障子や欄間が欠かせない。とくに障子を通す光は日本の家屋にとって最高の自然照明である。その意味でも障子を利用したいものだ。

Dining-conference room. A number of small tables can be
freely arranged to suit the immediate needs of the occasion.

会議室兼ダイニングルーム。

SITE PLAN

ABOVE: The bathhouse of the Union Bank of Switzerland Guesthouse is spectacular and reminiscent of a Japanese hot-spring resort. The floor of the bath itself is made from *izuishi* stone, and that of the changing room is natural rattan.

FAR LEFT: The stairway, as seen from the central corridor, is designed to enhance the openness of the interior.

LEFT: The corridor connecting the bathhouse to the main structure is based on a traditional garden footpath.

上：光がふりそそぐ開放的な湯殿。藤むしろを敷いた脱衣室から続く。左下：廊下側から階段を見る。右下：渡り廊下の飛び石。

RIGHT: Unlike *gassho zukuri* farmhouses, the main living rooms of this house have relatively low, flat ceilings and utilize decoratively carved transoms.

一階奥の間を通して西側の中庭を見る。建具を開け放つと広々とした空間になっている。

THE TAKANASHI HOUSE

A copper roof replaces the thatch while retaining the original shape

I received a commission to examine an old home within the grounds of Sakuragi Shrine in Noda City, Chiba Prefecture, from the chief priest, Mr. Itsuki Takanashi, and his family. They wanted me to completely rethink the dwelling and rebuild it more comfortably, from the main and sub-buildings through the *kura* storehouse, gates, bathhouse, and sheds. It is common for the owners of large, old houses in Japan to demolish them and replace them with something modern built from scratch. This deplorable practice is what motivated me to preserve *minka* in the first place, and I was very pleased to meet someone who wanted to restore the old buildings rather than destroy them.

Since the woods on the northern side were spreading and closing in on the main house and the storehouse, I shifted the buildings, foundations and all, to a new spot on the site. I changed the thatch of the beautiful main house to copper roofing, retaining the shape of the roof; put in subfloor heating and an air-conditioning unit hidden behind a wooden grille; and converted the shed to a garage. The sub-building, main house, storehouse, and the new bathhouse that I made were joined by corridors that gave the house a sense of unity. The project took four years to complete. Fortunately, a fine carpenter, Mr. Eishi Sanjo, did the work single-handedly. The Takanashi family's unwavering intention to pass on traditional Japanese culture to the next generation insured the success of this challenging project.

This renovation is not a *gassho zukuri* house, but a traditional ecclesiastical dwelling. It features three separate entryways (two of which are visible here), intended for visitors of different rank and for ceremonial usage.

外観。この屋根は合掌造りではない。正面玄関と中玄関へ続く道が美しい。

髙梨邸

茅葺き屋根を銅葺きにかえて屋根の形を保存

千葉県野田市の桜木神社内にある古い屋敷構えを、母屋、離れ、蔵、門、納屋、湯殿など総合的に見直し、住みやすく再構築するよう髙梨宮司とご家族から依頼を受けた。古くて広い屋敷の持ち主には、すっかり壊して新しい住居を建ててしまう人が多い。そんなときに私の仕事が必要とされるわけだが、古いまま生かそう、という人に出会ったのは嬉しかった。

まず、北側の林が南へと繁りだして母屋と蔵を圧迫していたので、土台ごと曳いて新しい位置に据えなおした。茅葺き屋根の美しい母屋を銅葺きにかえて屋根の形を残し、床暖房を入れエアコンを木の格子で隠し、納屋をガレージにした。移動した母屋と蔵、新しく作った湯殿、離れをそれぞれ廊下でつなぎ、家としての一体感をだす。完成までには5年の年月がかかった。幸い優れた大工の三條栄志さんがひとりで仕事をやりとげてくれたこと、髙梨宮司ご一家が最後まで日本の伝統文化を次の世代に引き継がせたいとの意志を貫いてくれたことで、この大きな仕事をやりとげることができた。

SITE PLAN

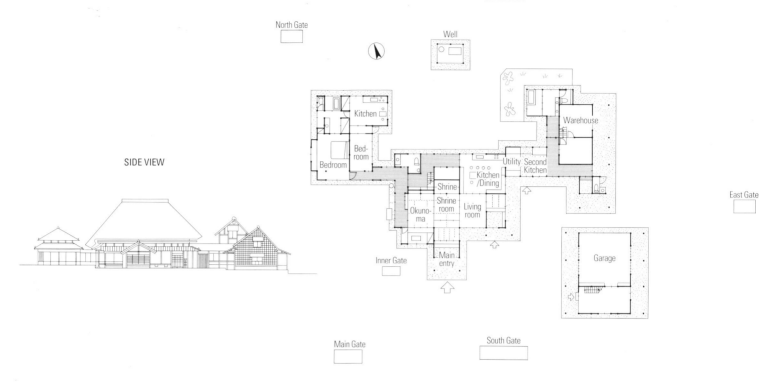

North Gate

Well

Kitchen

Warehouse

Bed-room

Bedroom

Utility

Second Kitchen

SIDE VIEW

East Gate

Shrine

Kitchen /Dining

Shrine room

Living room

Okuno-ma

Inner Gate

Garage

Main entry

Main Gate

South Gate

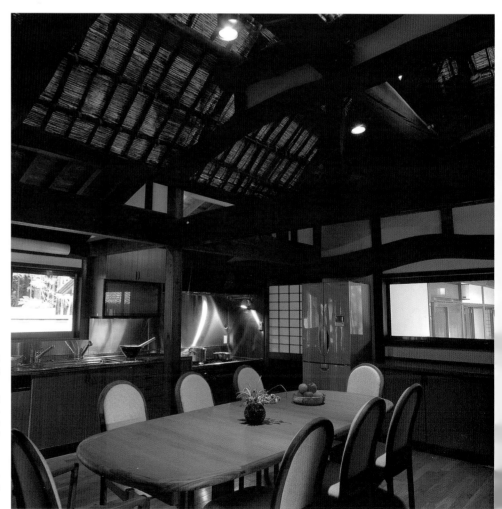

RIGHT: In the dining and kitchen area, fashioned from the original kitchen and service areas, the ceiling is open to the roof rafters.

FAR RIGHT: The house features a second kitchen, which is pressed into service during festivals and other occasions when large numbers of guests must be served. It has been left in its original location, though the former earthen floor has been replaced by a tile one.

下：天井を取りはらい空間をいかしたダイニングキッチン。
右：土間台所。キッチンから一段下がったスペース。行事や特殊な時に使われる。昔はここに竈が置かれていた。

ABOVE: The bath, located in a separate wing, has a handsome stone floor. The small garden has been carefully designed to maximize privacy.

BOTTOM RIGHT: A kind of reception room opens directly to the inner garden and allows intimate friends to visit informally.

上：坪庭を望む快適な湯殿。湯船は木曾石。下：正面玄関脇に作られた応接コーナー。

◀ PREVIOUS PAGE: The ceiling and roof structure are made of cedar, pine, and bamboo. While not identical to a *gassho zukuri*, the Takanashi House possesses a similar flavor.

前ページ：松と杉、竹で構成された天井。合掌天井とは違う別の美しさ。

CLOCKWISE, FROM TOP LEFT: The exterior of the *kura* storehouse, which has been moved and remade as a wing for a young couple.

The second-floor bedroom of the *kura*.

The *kura* bedroom, as seen from the second-floor lounge room.

左上：移動した蔵の外観。右上：蔵の二階は寝室になっている。
下：クラシックなインテリアがおしゃれな蔵の二階。

RIGHT: The raised central matted area allows a large number of guests to enjoy informal recitals.

広々とした一階居間。和室を囲む広間にはピアノが置かれ、リサイタルもできる。

THE OFUNA HOUSE
A 50-mat living room, spacious enough for concerts

The owner, who was planning to move from Tokyo, readied 600 *tsubo* (1,980 square meters/21,000 square feet) of land on one side of the mountain in Ofuna where the statue of the Ofuna Kannon is located. He asked me to build a large, spacious *gassho zukuri* house, so I brought two dwellings from Fukui Prefecture and combined them into one gabled building. I converted the roughly 25-*tsubo* (82.5-square-meters/900-square-foot) floor space of one dwelling to a big dining room and kitchen, and with the other dwelling I made a 33-mat-size Western-style sitting room with subfloor heating and a big 16-mat Japanese-style room. I connected the two rooms without using dividers of any sort so that they can be used as one big living room. The couple loves music, and I paid special attention to acoustics so they could enjoy their audio equipment to the fullest, and even hold concerts. On the second floor were rooms for the couple's daughters (who were studying abroad at the time), the master bedroom, and a guest room. For these rooms, I used new materials, taking care to give them a bright, modern feel.

The exterior, showing the large, tiled entry hall and the corridor which joins the two buildings.

外観。渡り廊下で左手の離れにつながる。

In the detached wing, which I built with new materials in the style of an old *minka* dwelling, I took a hint from Japanese open-air baths and gave the second-floor bathroom glass-walled views of the mountain on three sides. The glass-enclosed 20-meter (65-foot) corridor that connects the study and tatami room on the first floor with the main house forms a promenade, snaking through the shrubs and wild grasses of the rolling garden.

大船の家
コンサートもできる50畳のリビング

　東京から移住を予定していたT氏は、鎌倉の大船観音と同じ山の一隅に600坪の敷地を用意されていた。合掌民家を使ってゆったりと、大きな住まいをと希望されたので、福井県から民家二棟を運び、一つの切妻合掌の家に納めた。一棟分にあたる25坪ほどに、キッチンと広いダイニングを作り、もう一棟は33畳の床暖房を設けたフローリングと16畳の広い和室を、間仕切りの壁も建具も使わずワンルームとして使うリビングにした。音楽好きのご夫妻がオーディオを充分楽しめるよう、またコンサートの開催も可能なように音響効果を工夫した。二階は留学中の娘さんたちのための個室、夫妻の寝室、客室など新材を使って明るくモダンな部屋を心がけた。

　新材を民家風に古く見せて建てた離れには、二階に露天風呂を意識して裏山の自然を三方から眺める総ガラスの浴室を作った。一階の書斎、和室と母屋をつなぐ20mの渡り廊下は、遊歩道として総ガラスにし、起伏のある庭内の野草や樹木の間を縫うように伸びている。

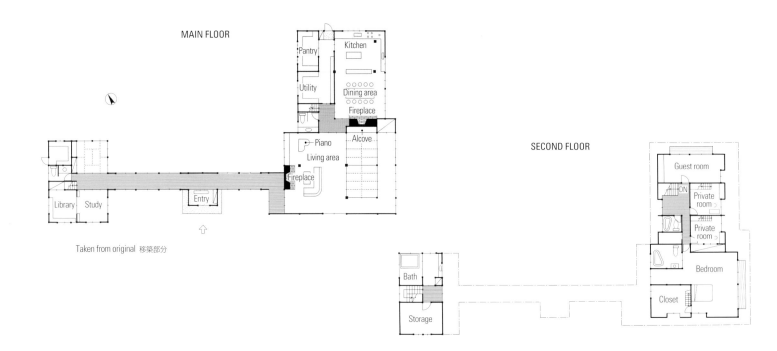

MAIN FLOOR

Pantry

Kitchen

Utility

Dining area

Fireplace

Piano

Alcove

Living area

Fireplace

Library

Study

Entry

Taken from original　移築部分

SECOND FLOOR

Guest room

Private room

Private room

Bedroom

Closet

Bath

Storage

FLOORING: Modern subfloor heating can be an immense help in miti-
gating the natural draftiness and chill of *minka*, but its use necessarily
limits the kinds of flooring materials that can be used. Heat causes natural, untreated wood to crack and warp, so despite their beauty, the
shining dark pine and zelkova floors that adorn old *minka* must be ruled
out. The option is to select heat-resistant flooring that looks as much
like wood as possible. Cork and tile are other possibilities, but for maxi-
mum warmth, rush matting is best. Cushioned flooring is water resistant
and easy to clean.

　　Tatami is falling steadily out of favor in Japan, but a reconstructed
minka should have at least one tatami room, however small. Slippers are
removed before entering, so the tatami stays clean, and the sensation of
walking barefoot on woven straw mats is a delightful link with the past.
The flexibility of tatami is another advantage: it is equally suited for a
parlor, study, tearoom, or bedroom. For these and many other reasons,
tatami deserves consideration.

床：快適な床暖房を入れるとおのずから床の材料は限られてくる。移築の場
合、熱のために自然の無垢の木はひび割れゆがんでしまうので、昔の黒光りす
る松や欅の美しい板は使えない。床暖房対応型の特殊なフローリングのなか
から、少しでも木の雰囲気のあるものを選ぶ。その他、コルク、タイルなども
あり、熱効率に関してはい草マットが最高である。また、水回りにはクッショ
ンフロアが水に強く掃除もしやすい。
畳は年々肩身が狭くなってきているが、民家移築では、小さくても一部屋は確
保したい。畳が敷いてある部屋にはスリッパも脱いで入るので清潔で、はだ
しで歩く感触は独特の気持ちよさがある。そのうえ、応接、書斎、茶の間、寝
室など多目的に使える点が素晴らしい。畳はもっと見直して良いと思う。

FACING PAGE: The living room of the Ofuna House.

BELOW: A spacious counter separates the dining area from the kitchen,
which itself is arranged around a large butcher-block worktable.

左ページ：居間のコーナーには骨董が飾られている。下：ゆったりとしたダイニングコー
ナー。キッチンとの境には低めの棚を配し、庭の景色も楽しめる快適なスペース。

COUNTERCLOCKWISE, FROM TOP LEFT: The bathroom features a Western-style clawfoot bathtub and is generally arranged in American fashion.

The master bedroom is on the second floor in a section of the house which was built entirely new. The ceiling is boarded.

The connecting corridor, looking toward the living area. The floor is comprised of twenty-three tatami mats and affords an exquisite light-filled procession from one wing to the other.

上：アメリカンスタイルの二階バスルーム。猫足の湯船が楽しい。
下：床暖房つきの二階主寝室。新しい木材を使った白木の合掌屋根裏は、明るく清潔感があり爽快である。右：長い渡り廊下は部屋の感覚で使われていて、障子を通した光に包まれて離れへと続いている。

HALLS: In a traditional *minka*, the veranda runs alongside the tatami room, serving as a corridor. During reconstruction, it is often enclosed and made into a room. Constructing a new hallway is rarely necessary, because the veranda is usually well placed to connect the living room, entryway, or stairway hall to the other rooms while preserving the atmosphere of the *minka*. In the case of detached buildings, using a walkway or gallery to connect them to the main house allows the outdoors to be incorporated nicely into the design of the house and is recommended wherever conditions permit doing so.

廊下：移築前の民家には座敷に沿って縁側があり、廊下の役目も果たしていたが、移築するときその部分を室内に取り込み一部屋にするケースが多い。移築であらためて廊下を作ったのは一軒のみだ。民家の雰囲気を保つためには、むしろ居間とか玄関や階段ホールから次の部屋につなげるほうが無理がないからである。ただし、母屋と別棟をつなぐような廊下や回廊は、自然との一体感を感じさせる演出効果もあるので、土地の環境が許せば積極的に計画したい。

The master bath, on the second floor. Also part of the newly built section, this bath is light-filled and made of aromatic wood. The tub holds four people.

離れの二階に作られた露天風呂のようなバスルーム。自然に包まれて無垢の槇の風呂桶につかると快適このうえない。

BATHS AND TOILETS: In 1976, when I reconstructed a *minka* for my own use as a combined home and gallery, I put a toilet on the second floor but, fearing leaks, not a bath. Today's advanced waterproofing technology means that second-floor baths are no longer a problem in Japan. Columns and beams must be sturdy enough to support the weight, however, and soundproofing is almost as necessary as waterproofing. Modern living practically demands baths and toilets adjacent to the sleeping areas.

If placing a bath and toilet on the first floor proves difficult, a small addition can be made. The fact that such an addition will project a bit away from the main body of the house makes it possible to surround it with a garden and at the same time minimize or eliminate problems of sound, odor, and dampness. More ambitiously, an outdoor, hotspring–style bath in a detached building which is accessible by a covered walkway can be built, allowing bathers to enjoy the delights of nature. The Japanese bath is said to embody the essence of Japanese culture, and as a cultural and personal expression, it presents endless design possibilities.

浴室とトイレ：1976年、自宅兼ギャラリー用に民家を移築するとき、二階にトイレは設けたが、浴室は水漏れが心配で計画しなかった。今は防水工事の技術が非常に進んだので、二階に浴室を作っても大丈夫になった。ただし、何トンにもなる重量に耐える柱と梁があることと、防水だけでなく防音工事にも十分な注意を払う必要がある。寝室に隣接する浴室やトイレは、快適な住まい作りに欠かせない時代になってきた。一階の浴室、トイレを母屋の内部に設けるのが困難な場合、下屋を出すことによってスペースを確保する。母屋から少し突出するので、自然を取り込みやすくなり、音、臭い、湿気の処理を考えると一石二鳥だ。この計画を拡大すると、別棟に小さな湯殿を建てて渡り廊下でつなぐ温泉風露天風呂も可能で、自然を満喫できる。風呂は日本文化の凝縮といわれる。風呂作りの夢は尽きない。

RIGHT: The living room provides cozy country-
style living in the middle of Tokyo's bustle.

一階居間。大都市の一角とは思えない閑静な空間。

THE MUSASHINO HOUSE
Two skylights in the attic and a moon-viewing room

There was a two-year delay after I received the commission for the Musashino House, which was built in á Tokyo residential area, and the start of building. The actual construction took a further one-and-a-half years. It was, in fact, a particularly busy period, when I had several overlapping projects, but my excitement at the prospect of building a house in one of Tokyo's most famous residential areas, coupled with my wish to fulfill the couple's vision of their home down to the smallest details, meant that I felt the need to devote considerable attention to the project. The owner's wife possessed a number of treasures, including a figure of Buddha that had been passed down from her parents. It was a memorable experience for me to be shown these pieces in advance, and to be asked to design the rooms around them.

Since there was a height restriction on the plot, I used only the upper section of the dwelling I had brought from Fukui Prefecture, as a *gassho* gabled roof. The portion that had been the kitchen became the living room; the mezzanine floor served as a lounge and storage space; the second floor housed a bedroom, shower room, and library. The top floor, in accordance with the owner's wife's wishes, became a "moon-viewing room." The moon can be seen through two skylights I built on the ends of the *gassho* beams. I also had the idea of soundproofing the house by making the walls and floors thicker, and the technique of using 5-*sun* (about 15-centimeter/6-inch) timbers for the external pillars successfully lent a feeling of solidity and stability. This house can be considered a compilation of all my work up to that point.

武蔵野の家
屋根裏に天窓二つ、月見の間

　東京吉祥寺の住宅街に建てた武蔵野の家は依頼があってから二年待っていただき、着工から一年半かかって完成した。仕事が重なり多忙な時期でもあったが、東京の代表的な住宅地に建てるという意気込みと、ご夫妻の住まいに対する明確なヴィジョンや細部の具体的な注文に応えたいという気持ちから、力をつくした。夫人には、ご両親から譲られたという仏像をはじめ、大切にされている所蔵品がいくつかあった。こうした品をあらかじめ示されて、それに合わせて部屋を設計するという貴重な体験もした。

　敷地の制約があったので福井から移築した民家のジョウヤ（上屋）のみを切妻合掌として使い、台所だった部分にリビングを、中二階にラウンジと納戸、二階に寝室とシャワールーム、書庫、そして屋根裏には夫人の希望で「月見の間」を作った。合掌の突っ先に天窓を二つ作っての月見である。

　床と壁を厚くして防音につとめ、側柱にすべて五寸柱を使って安定感、重量感をだす工夫なども成功した。この家は、私の仕事の集大成の感がある。

SECTION THROUGH

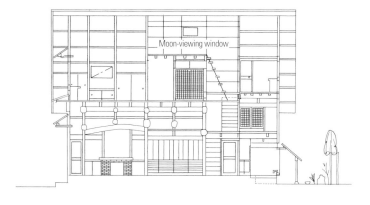

Moon-viewing window

MAIN FLOOR

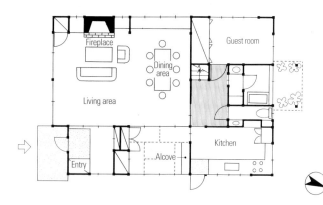

Fireplace

Dining area

Living area

Guest room

Kitchen

Entry

Alcove

Taken from original 移築部分

SECOND FLOOR

Storage Storage Closet

Bedroom

Library

Bedroom

Shower

In the dining room, the fine nineteenth-century folding screen and traditional Shinto household shrine (upper left) harmonize well with replicas of English antiques.

一階居間のダイニングコーナー。英国製の家具に19世紀の屏風、行灯が古民家にみごとに似合っている。

FAR LEFT: The mezzanine space is furnished as a comfortable lounge, with a Chinese rosewood table, an antique chaise lounge, a large chest from Sado Island, and a beautiful folding-screen painting of plover.

LEFT AND BELOW: Two bedrooms in natural tones. The larger one has a natural bare-wood finish.

左：中二階ラウンジ。佐渡箪笥に千鳥の屏風を配して、ギャラリーのような雰囲気になっている。上：二階北側の寝室は夫人のプライベートスペース。下：白木のインテリアが美しい二階主寝室。

LEFT AND ABOVE: The third-floor attic is now a poetic moon-viewing room with skylights.

The main stair landing has a pair of display alcoves and a sliding-screen window.

左：屋根裏に作られた月見の間。天窓から月を見る遊びのスペース。上：中二階の踊り場。

The owner refers to the main bathing area on the first floor as a private hot-spring bath. The design borrows from traditional open-air baths, with large openable windows facing a small garden. The floor is granite, and the tub, cypress.

武蔵野温泉と名付けられた坪庭付きのバスルーム。檜の浴槽と御影石を使い、贅沢なひとときを楽しむ。

chapter 6

INTERIOR DESIGN
AND ANTIQUES

PREVIOUS PAGE: Six-panel folding screen with nature scene, late-Edo period; Sendai *ikken* chest, zelkova, Meiji period; gourd-shaped bamboo basket; deer incense burner, bronze, late Edo period.

前ページ：花鳥図屏風、六曲紙本金地彩色（江戸前期）。欅仙台一間単笥（明治）。ひょうたん型竹籠。鹿のブロンズ香炉（江戸後期）。

The undecorated interior of any traditional residential structure in Japan—not only *gassho zukuri*—has a finished beauty of its own. Even on ceremonial occasions in the main room, decoration is spare: a single scroll painting hanging in the alcove, an arrangement of flowers, an incense burner. In the old days, the Japanese lived without chairs, so introducing sofas and chairs into a reconstructed *minka* naturally transforms the interior design.

In 1977, after my own residence was ready to inhabit, I pondered what sort of furnishings would best suit its wide interior, with dark beams and rafters like massive pieces of sculpture. On a trip to the Hokuriku area, I went into an antique store and discovered a zelkova storehouse door so heavy that four men could barely lift it. On the spur of the moment I decided to fashion legs for it and use it as living-room table—a happy inspiration as it turned out, since the table goes perfectly with the ambiance of the room and never fails to attract the admiration of visitors. Next I needed chairs. When the head of the Tokyo branch of Fiat ended his term of office and was heading home, he let me have a set of leather-covered chairs made in England. Deep down I was far from sure they would look right in an old *minka*, but to my relief they blended well with the door-table. Little by little I came to see that French and Italian furniture, as well as chairs and sofas from the Meiji (1868–1912) and Taisho (1912–26) eras that were designed for Western-style parlors, also would work. Who knows, maybe something in the dirt-floor entrance and kitchen area of an old Japanese farmhouse is intrinsically Western.

Chairs, of course, alter what is "eye level" in the room. Since most old Japanese objects were designed to be used or appreciated while sitting on the floor, looking down on them from a chair is not a good idea. I raised them to eye level by constructing a counter along the window, at an appropriate distance from the floor. Raising an antique screen slightly off the floor by hanging it on the wall also proved effective, lending a welcome touch of elegance to the rustic interior. Another interesting way to decorate the limited wall space of a traditional Japanese house is to frame old *fusuma-e* (paintings on paper-covered sliding panels) and hanging scroll-paintings in appropriate sizes at the eye level of Western-style paintings.

But no matter how much care is lavished on objects, without proper lighting the effect will be ruined. To bring out the distinctive appeal of columns and beams, indirect lighting is best, with the source of the light tucked away out of sight. Generous use of spotlighting can also make the interior come alive, and wonderful effects can be gained using *washi*, handmade Japanese paper. Light shining from old-fashioned paper-covered lamp stands (*andon*) or filtering in through translucent sliding doors (*shoji*) is not only soft and flattering to art objects, but envelops people in a gentle warmth like that of firelight in a fireplace.

Old folk objects go well with traditional-style houses. Antique wooden chests, once crafted all over Japan with a rich variety of design, not only are useful for storage but can be enjoyed as well for the beauty of their grain, metal fittings, and embellishments. They can also be used as a sideboard to display objects or hold an antique lampstand. Like traditional houses themselves, the more such chests are cared for, the more they increase in "beauty of utility."

A *minka* itself may be seen as a giant antique; indeed, what could be better to display antiques in than an antique house? Now and then I like to alter the arrangement, whether for a special occasion or on a sudden whim; either way, I find it is both fun and educational, never failing to yield some unexpected insight. If you use your imagination in thinking of ways to use and display antiques, you are bound to find some that are cheaper and of better quality than their modern equivalents. Anyone who lives day to day with Japanese antiques can't help feeling respect and gratitude for the wisdom and achievement of earlier generations, thereby rediscovering the value of traditional Japanese life.

合掌造りに限らず日本の伝統的な家屋は、飾り物がなくてもそのままで完成した美しい空間となっている。冠婚葬祭に使われる座敷ですら床の間に掛け軸1本、生花に香炉があるだけという極めて簡素なインテリアだ。昔は椅子のない生活であったので、移築した民家に椅子やソファを持ち込むようになると、インテリアは自然と変わってくる。

自宅を完成した1977年、柱や梁が黒々と力強く彫刻のように見える広い内部にどんな家具を持ち込もうかと探していたところ、旅先の北陸の古道具屋で、四人でやっと持ち上げられるほど

の重くて頑丈な欅の蔵戸を見つけた。まったくの思いつきだったが、この古い蔵戸に脚を作り、リビングのテーブルにしてみたところ、思いのほかぴったりで、来客の注目の的となった。次に椅子は、FIATの東京支社長が任期を終えて帰国される時、それまで使っておられた英国製の革張りの椅子を譲っていただきこれを使ってみた。内心古い民家に合うかどうか不安であったが、蔵戸のテーブルの前で違和感なくほっとした。フランス製やイタリア製も、それに洋風応接間のために作られた明治、大正頃の椅子やソファもよく調和することがだんだん判ってきた。民家の土間やダイドコの部分には意外と洋風な要素があるのかもしれない。

さて、椅子の生活になると「目線」は当然変わってくる。古来、日本の「モノ」は座して使ったり鑑賞したりするようにデザインさ

れている場合が多いので、椅子から見下ろすことになると具合が悪い。窓際に設けたカウンターの上など、床より高いので程良い「目線」になるし、時代屏風も床より少し上げて壁に飾ると、素朴な民家にエレガントな雰囲気がでて魅力ある空間ができる。また民家に少ない壁面を飾るには、古い襖絵、掛け軸など古画を適当なサイズに額装して洋風の目線で飾ると面白い効果がだせると思う。

しかし、どんなに努力して物を飾ってみても照明の方法を間違えると台無しになる。建物の柱や梁の持ち味を生かすためには、照明器具をむき出しにせずなるべく隠すようにする間接照明が適している。スポットライトなども多用するとインテリアが生きてくる。また和紙を通す光も見逃せない。障子を通して入ってくる光や古い行灯の灯も柔らかで美術品に効果的であるばかりでなく、暖炉の火の光とともに人をやさしく包んでくれる。

民家には古い民芸品がよく似合う。昔日本各地で作られた意匠豊かな時代タンスなどは、収納として役に立つばかりかインテリアの一つとしても、その木目や金具など楽しめる。またサイドボードのようにタンスの上に物を飾ったり時代行灯を置いたりもできる。民家と同じで、タンスは手入れをすればするほど「用の美」が増すように思える。

民家はそれ自体大きな骨董品といえる。骨董の家には骨董品がよく似合うと思う。置き場所を時により気分により変えてみるのも楽しく、そのつど新しい発見があり学ぶことは多い。使い方や飾り方を工夫すれば、なかには現代物より安くて上質なものに出会うことがある。こうして日常、骨董品と暮らしていると、自然に先人の知恵と努力に敬意と感謝の気持ちをもち、日本の良さを再発見するようになると思う。

FOLDING SCREENS 屏風

BELOW: Six-panel screen, pine and bamboo, mid-Edo period.

FACING PAGE, CLOCKWISE FROM TOP LEFT: Low six-panel screen, mid-Edo period. *Falcons*, by Fujiwara Masayoshi, framed panels from a folding screen. 1740. Low six-panel screen with chrysanthemums, mid-Edo period. Six-panel screen with crows, mid-Edo period.

下：松に滝の図屏風、六曲紙本金地彩色（江戸中期）。右ページ左上：花鳥図枕屏風、六曲紙本金地彩色（江戸中期）。右上：鷹の図額絵一対、紙本彩色（藤原政吉1740年）六曲張り混ぜ屏風を額装する。左下：烏の図屏風、六曲紙本金砂子墨絵（江戸中期）。右下：菊の図枕屏風、六曲金地彩色（江戸中期）。

TANSU CHESTS AND LANTERNS　箪笥と照明

RIGHT: Lantern, Enshu-style, red lacquer and paper; money chest, zelkova, Echizen Prefecture, late Edo period.

BOTTOM LEFT: Small chest, zelkova, Iwate Prefecture, late Edo period.

BOTTOM RIGHT: Medicine chest, paulownia, late Edo period; porcelain vase, Old Imari.

FACING PAGE: Chest on wheels, Yamagata Prefecture, Meiji period; square lantern, Meiji period; Japanese antique carpet, Hyogo Prefecture, Meiji period.

右：朱漆円周行灯。欅帳場箪笥、越前（江戸後期）。左下：欅小箪笥、岩手（江戸後期）。
花竹籠（明治）。右下：総桐薬箪笥（江戸後期）。古伊万里の白磁の壺に生け花。
右ページ：欅車箪笥、山形（明治）。角行灯（明治）。赤穂緞通（明治）。

IMARI PORCELAIN AND BAMBOO BASKETRY
伊万里と竹籠

TOP RIGHT: Large plate, blue-and-white porcelain with arabesque pattern, Old Imari, late-Edo period.

BOTTOM LEFT: Bamboo basket with tree-root handle, Meiji period.

BOTTOM RIGHT: Bamboo basket, Meiji period.

右：染め付け古伊万里ひねり唐草紋様大皿（江戸後期）。下：花竹籠（明治）、木の根を使った柄。自然の不思議な形が魅力的。右下：花竹籠（明治）彫刻のようなオブジェとして飾る。

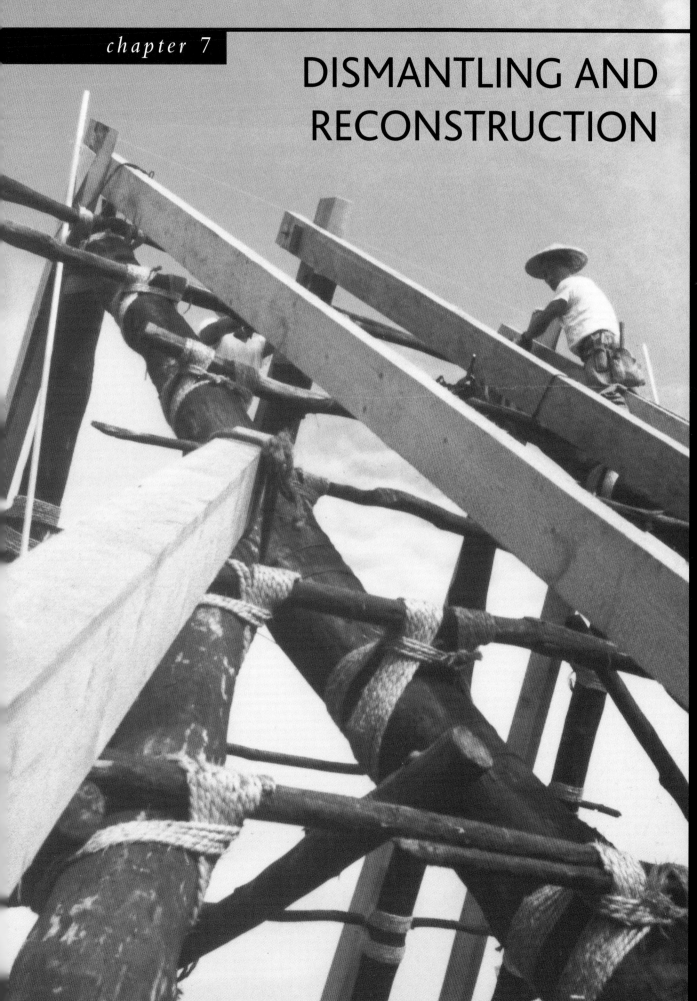

chapter 7

DISMANTLING AND RECONSTRUCTION

To date, I have dismantled about fifty dwellings for transfer and reconstruction, and the process is always roughly the same.

First, I make a record. As well as taking photos and measurements and drawing up an accurate plan, I also ask the owner for stories relating to the house and the village. These are duly recorded. The photos are not so much for reference during the reconstruction as to let the new owner see the dwelling in its original form. This is because it is often difficult to schedule a visit to the site with the customer before dismantling. The task of measuring is generally carried out by two people, and climbing on the beams and crawling about under the roof of a big *gassho zukuri* house, black with soot, is not easy work. Furthermore, the drawing up of accurate plans is a terribly important and difficult task. Since the spaces have been lived in for a long time, it is only natural that there are lots of things that can get in the way, and alterations over the years often mean that the original form of the pillars and beams is not visible.

Next, the work schedule must be decided. Early spring, from March to April, when there is still some snow on the ground, is the preferred time for dismantling, particularly for disposing of the roofing thatch, which takes place first. The large quantity of thatch is bundled up with help from farmers, moved to a safe place and burned on top of the remaining snow. I am told that the ash that results makes good fertilizer. The organic nature of the thatch ash, as well as most of the other waste that emerges from the demolition process, means that it is relatively safe and that it conveniently decomposes over time in a natural manner.

Things that are invariably stored away at the time of dismantling include the rafter materials; the Japanese cedar logs used for the main frame and so on; beams; pillars; *sashikamoi* and so forth; plus the bamboo and other materials from the ceiling. Panels from the walls and floor are, with the exception of some pine and zelkova wood, generally discarded. Wooden doors and the like are sometimes retained, but as the dimensions often do not fit the new house, they frequently cannot be reused.

The dismantling process proceeds with the help of cranes and other machines. As the soot-stained beams and pillars are laid bare, the timbers, which have watched over the passing of centuries and generations of lives, stand dignified, their duties complete. Having been transformed into something of a mysterious, forbidding object, these pillars and beams await a new breath of life.

Once the waste from the dismantling has been disposed of, the materials from the dwelling are transported to the storage site. Before the work of reassembly can begin in earnest, there are other jobs to be done, and everything is stored in the meantime in a warehouse on my worksite in the town of Shirotori. The main supports of dwellings from areas of heavy snowfall are often massive timbers measuring 10 or 15 meters (36 or 52 feet) in length and sometimes weighing several tons. As there are also long curved beams and other unwieldy elements, loading them onto trucks is no easy task. When one considers the road regulations regarding weight and size limits, it is a real headache.

The greatest concern during storage is to ensure that a natural breeze can move between the stacked timbers, to keep the wood dry enough to prevent rot. It also goes without saying that direct sunlight and rain are to be avoided. Once, I had a marten build a nest among some stored timbers. Another time, I lifted some timbers only to have a swarm of insects suddenly fly out, the stored wood having become a giant nesting area. I always keep several dismantled dwellings in storage to meet orders

A *minka* before removal.
移築直前の橋本嘉兵衛邸（29代）福井県

With the roof and walls removed, an impressive horizontal beam is exposed to view.

屋根をおろし下屋を取り払うと巨大な梁が現れる。

私は過去に民家を50棟ほど移築目的で解体したが、そのプロセスはほぼ同じである。

まず初めに記録をとる。写真を撮り、寸法を測って正確な図面を作成するほか、持ち主から家や村にまつわる物語などを聞き書きする。写真は民家再生の時の参考にするためというより、施主（移築依頼主）に民家の元の姿を見てもらうためのものである。施主に解体前に現地に行って見てもらうのはタイミングからいって難しい場合が多いからだ。寸法を採る作業は通常二人で行うのだが、煤で真っ黒になった合掌造りの屋根裏にもぐり梁に昇ったりするのは、あまり楽な仕事ではない。また図面を正確に作成するのは大変重要な作業であるが、なかなか難しい作業でもある。生活の場であったために当然ながら物がたくさんあって寸法を採る邪魔になったり、長い年月のうちに改造され柱とか梁の元の姿が見えない場合もある。

次に作業日の決定である。解体は残雪のまだ残る春先、3月から4月にかけてするのが望ましい。大仕事である屋根の茅をおろし処分するのに好都合なのだ。まず屋根の茅をおろすと、大量の茅は農家の人たちの手を借りて束ね、安全な場所に移し、残雪の上で燃やす。この時出る灰は農作物のための良い肥料になるという。茅の灰ばかりでなく古民家から出る大量の不要物は、もともと自然の材料を使っているので安心でもあり、時が経てば自然に還り土となるという合理性をもっている。

解体の時必ず保管するものは、合掌材、軸組構造材などの杉丸太、柱、梁、差鴨居、天井材の煤竹などである。板壁や床板は、欅材、松材の一部以外は処分される場合が多い。板戸などは一部保管されることもあるが、寸法が合わないといった理由で結局移築時には使用されないことが多い。

今はクレーンなど機械の助けを借りて、このような工程で解体が進み、煤で真っ黒になった柱と梁が全容を現わすと、何百年の時の流れと人々の生活の営みを見守ってきた木材が、その責務を果たし終えて凛と建っている。一種近寄り難い神秘的な物体にさえ思えてくる。民家移築とはこの柱や梁に新しい息吹きを与えることなのだ。

解体時に出たゴミを処理した後、次は材料として姿を変えた民家を保管場所へ運搬する。本格的に移築するまでにはまだ手を加える作業があり、それまで白鳥町にある作業場の一画にある倉庫

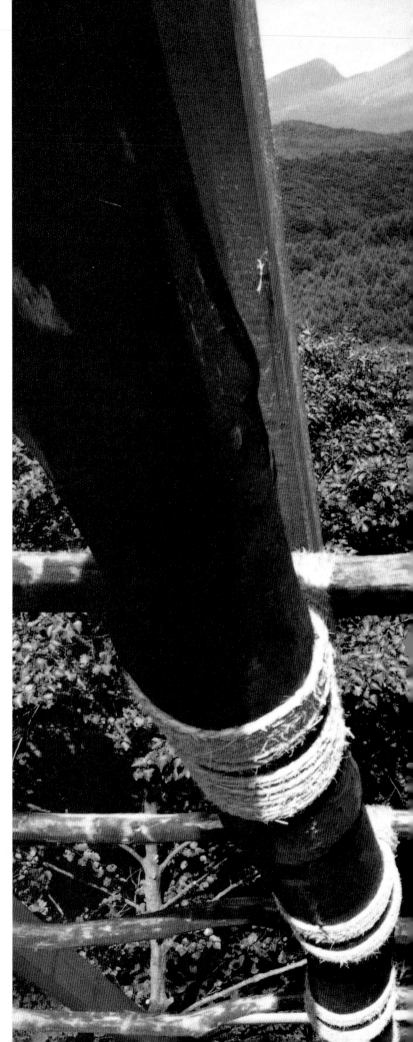

from customers. Once I have received an order, I listen to the client's requests and present a basic plan and a rough estimate. These buildings are technologically simple, but so different from contemporary residences that it is sometimes difficult to describe the reconstruction process, including its beauty, to clients. It takes a great deal longer than simply building a new modern house, and circumstances can change during that time, sometimes leading to misunderstandings, great and small. I think that the most important thing is to establish a relationship of trust between the client and myself as director of the project. Only then can our shared image be translated into reality. I usually use the first house I rebuilt, that of my foster father in Kamakura, as a model and a stage upon which to build a concrete image. Then, together, the client and I move the discussion along, offering each other new ideas as we proceed.

Once the contract has been signed, the materials are brought out of the storage space and onto the bare earth of my worksite in Shirotori.

The worksite, including a workshop, storehouse, and the test assembly site, covers about 600 *tsubo* (1,980 square meters/21,330 square feet), and it is here that the preliminary work for the reassembly takes place. In the workshop, damaged pillars and beams are restored, replacements and repairs are made with aged timbers of the same kind of wood, and other similar jobs are carried out. In the storehouse, unused timber from other dismantled houses is kept and can be used for replacements—new mortises and tenons being cut where necessary. Everything required for the reconstruction is checked or restored in this workshop. The outdoor earthen plot is where the job of setting up the preliminary framework (*karigumi*) takes place. Old and new timbers are fitted together as they will actually be arranged, and after careful measurements are taken, a new blueprint is drawn up, and adjustments are made as necessary. The framework of the house at this point is nearly complete but will be dismantled again to be moved to its final location.

While this task is proceeding on the worksite, the preliminary foundations (*beta kiso*) are being prepared on the actual construction site. The weight of the heavy *gassho zukuri* structure requires the pouring of deep concrete foundations throughout.

When the foundation is finished, the *karigumi* is dismantled once again, and all the materials are taken from the worksite to the actual building site. After that, it is just a matter of putting everything together correctly once again on the new site. Being a special type of architecture, however, the job takes about ten months even for a carpenter who is well versed in *gassho zukuri*. Four or five Shirotori craftsmen, experienced in this kind of work, will go to the site, wherever it may be. Although there is

に保管される。豪雪地帯の民家の軸組は長さ10mから15mにおよぶ巨材が多く、重さも数百kgにおよぶ物もあり、また曲った長い梁などもあるため、トラックに積み込むのは生やさしい作業ではない。重量や長さの制限規制などを考慮すると頭の痛い仕事である。

　保管で一番気を遣うのは、積み込んである材料に自然の風が通るようにすることだ。いうまでもなく直射日光や雨は避けなければならない。ある時保管中にイタチの仲間であるテンという動物が材木の間に巣を作って住みついたことがあった。また昆虫が大量の卵を産みつけて開けてみたら虫の大群がワッと飛び出してきたという失敗もあった。

　こうして施主からの注文に対応すべく、つねにいくつかの解体された民家が保管されているわけである。施主から注文を受けると、相手方の希望を聞き、基本設計を提示、概算をだす。しかし現代住宅とはまったく異なり、原始的とも思える素朴な古い民家について、その移築再生の過程や魅力を、感覚的にわかっていただくのはそう簡単なことではない。新築よりはるかに長い年月がかかるため、その間に状況が変化して多少の誤解が生じることも皆無とはいえない。　いちばん大切なのは施主とプロデューサーである私との間の信頼関係をいかに築いていくかだと思う。その上でおたがいに共通するイメージを実現させていくのである。私の場合、鎌倉に最初に移築した養父ロデリックの家をモデルハウスとし、その舞台で具体的イメージを創っていく。そして個々のディテールについてまで、新しいアイディアをだしあいながら事を運んでいくのである。

　契約が成立すると、保管されている倉庫から材料が作業場の土場に引き出される。

　約600坪ある作業場の敷地には工作室、倉庫、土場があり、ここで移築までの下準備をする。工作室では、傷んでいる柱や梁を補修したり、同類の古材、たとえば欅だったものはほかの欅に取りかえるなどの作業が行われる。倉庫にはこれまで解体して未使用だった古材が保管されており、必要に応じて取りかえられるが、その場合あらためてホゾ、ホゾ穴なども設計に応じここで削られる。このほか移築に必要なすべてのチェックや補修をこの作業所で行う。土場というのは野外の広場で、ここでは「仮組」という作業を行う。古材や新材を組み立てて実際に構造を作りあげ、正確な採寸をした上で新しい設計図のもと修正個所があれば修正するわけである。

　作業場でこの作業が進行している間に、一方移築予定地では「ベタ基礎」という基盤作りが行われる。これは、重い合掌造り移築の住宅が耐えられるように、厚いコンクリートを一面に流し込んで作る基礎である。

Through the freshly lashed structure of a *gassho zukuri* roof, a view of Mount Asama.

組み終えた合掌屋根から浅間山を望む。

163

Various stages of rebuilding.
移築風景。

some variation according to the size of the house, in most cases about two years will pass from the time the first basic plans are drawn until completion.

When the *gassho zukuri* house is finally completed, the first problem to be considered is lighting. Brightness and openness are the primary selling points of contemporary housing in Japan, and the stark white illumination of fluorescent lights is preferred. However, this would overpower the subdued tones of the beams and *susudake* bamboo of these old houses. I really think the warmth of incandescent lamps is the most suitable. I place indirect light sources in locations where the fittings themselves will not stand out too much, simulating the atmosphere of the days when people lived by natural light. Putting lamps with *washi* shades (which give off a warm light through the Japanese paper) in odd corners of the room will help create a tranquil atmosphere.

Shortly after moving into a converted *gassho zukuri* dwelling, my clients often notice mysterious noises at night. Usually this is the creaking of the wood, and it causes one to feel that the house has really been reborn.

このベタ基礎ができあがると「仮組」は再びほどかれ、白鳥の作業場からすべての資材が移築現場に運びだされる。あとは現場で順序よく組み立てられるだけである。といっても特殊建築であり、合掌造りに精通した大工さんの手でもざっと10ヵ月ほどかかる作業である。通常この作業をよく知る白鳥の職人4、5名がどこの現場であろうと出向いて作業することになっている。家の大小で多少の差はあるものの、基本設計から数えると2年近くの歳月が経っている場合が多い。

こうして完成にこぎつけた合掌造りの住宅でまっさきに考えなければならないのは、照明の問題である。今の住宅では、明るく開放的というのが売り物になっており、蛍光灯の白っぽい光線が使われる。しかしそれでは梁や煤竹の落ち着いた色調をこわしてしまう。やはり白熱灯の暖かみのある光が適しているように思える。自然光で生きてきた昔のように、照明機器が主張しすぎないよう、間接照明を随所に使ったり、和紙を通して温かい光を送ってくれる行灯などを部屋の片隅に置けば、静謐な雰囲気がただようのではないだろうか。

現代住宅として再生された合掌造りの家に入居して間もないころは、夜など一種神秘的とも思える音が聞えることがある。木のきしむ音だろうか、そんな時、家が生き返ったと実感したりする。

LIST OF WORKS 今までの仕事

Date	Architecture	Location	Total Square Meters (Square Feet)	Page Reference
1967	Roderick House ローデリック邸	Kamakura 鎌倉	293 (3,153)	30
1975	Salomon Villa サロモン邸	Karuizawa 軽井沢	231 (2,486)	60
1976	Takishita House / House of Antiques, West Gallery (House of Antiques established in 1971) 瀧下邸／ハウス・オブ・アンティックス（1971年設立），ウエストギャラリー	Kamakura 鎌倉	284 (3,056)	40
1976-77	Karuizawa Villa 軽井沢の別荘	Karuizawa 軽井沢	363 (3,906)	66
1977-78	Amakasu House 甘糟邸	Kamakura 鎌倉	132 (1,420)	74
1978	David Kidd, Ashiya House (dismantled) デヴィッド・キッド邸（解体）	Ashiya 芦屋	396 (4,261)	
1979	Imai House 今井邸	Suwa 諏訪	321 (3,454)	
1979-80	Weber House ウェーバー邸	Hayama 葉山	330 (3,551)	80
1980-81	Kaiko-Tei (restaurant) 懐古亭	Kamakura 鎌倉	318 (3,422)	
1981-82	Omura House & Studio 大村邸&アトリエ	Kamakura 鎌倉	363 (3,906)	86
1981-84	Bierregard House & Folk Museum ビエレガード邸&博物館	Buenos Aires ブエノスアイレス	850 (9,146)	
1982-83	A Stone Sculptor's House & Studio 空邸&スタジオ	Takamatsu 高松	330 (3,551)	
1983-84	Tagawa Villa 田川邸	Hakone 箱根	264 (2,841)	92
1984-85	Sakurai House & Frame Shop 桜井邸&文海堂	Kamakura 鎌倉	429 (4,616)	
1984-86	Akiyama House 秋山邸	Zushi 逗子	531 (5,714)	98
1984-86	Rusty London, Hawaii House ラスティ・ロンドン，ハワイ邸	Honolulu ホノルル	785 (8,447)	
1985-86	Kuwata House 桑田邸	Kita Kamakura 北鎌倉	165 (1,775)	
1986-87	Korver House コーバー邸	Zushi 逗子	248 (2,668)	106
1986-87	Hayashi House 林邸	Sagamiko 相模湖	429 (4,616)	112
1987	Ohara Tea House (dismantled) 小原邸茶室（解体）	Ashiya 芦屋	16 (172)	
1987-88	Annex to Roderick House ローデリック邸増築	Kamakura 鎌倉	247 (2,658)	
1987-88	House of Antiques, East Gallery ハウス・オブ・アンティックス，イーストギャラリー	Kamakura 鎌倉	336 (3,615)	52
1987-89	Union Bank of Switzerland Guesthouse スイス・ユニオン銀行ゲストハウス	Yamanakako 山中湖	330 (3,551)	120
1990	Jomyoji Temple Tea House (design) 浄妙寺・茶室（設計）	Kamakura 鎌倉	148 (1,592)	
1990-2001	Takanashi House (for Shinto priest family) 髙梨邸	Noda 野田	198 (2,130) / 533 (5,735)	126
1990-2001	Ofuna House 大船の家	Ofuna 大船	788 (8,479) / 95 (1,022)	134
1991-95	Sakuragi Shrine Guesthouse & Office 桜木神社社務所&参集殿	Chiba 千葉	931 (10,018)	
1993-97	Oshima House 大島邸	Yokosuka 横須賀	248 (2,668)	
1998-99	Musashino House 武蔵野の家	Tokyo 東京	310 (3,336)	142
1999-2001	House of Antiques, South Gallery ハウス・オブ・アンティックス，サウスギャラリー	Kamakura 鎌倉	180 (1,937)	

AFTERWORD

It was thirty years ago, when I was twenty-one, that dam construction was scheduled to submerge Izumi village and I had one of its traditional *gassho zukuri* farmhouses removed and reconstructed in the hills of Kamakura, where I opened a store selling Imari ware and old folk objects. Begun as a young man's passing whim, the store owes much of its success to geographical serendipity: it is just the right distance from Tokyo, not too near and not too far. Visitors have included a rich and colorful assortment of VIPs from around the world—diplomats and businessmen, members of royalty, opera singers, artists. All without exception have expressed great interest in the building, telling me things like, "What a truly restful place this is," or "I could go on sitting here forever." The declaration of Mike Mansfield, then U.S. ambassador to this country, is etched in my mind: "Here is Japan." In 1984, I was elated when the owner of a stately mansion in California came to my store and fell in love with it, making an offer to swap.

Requests to have houses removed and rebuilt elsewhere came in largely from Westerners at first, so that as it developed, my work has been reflected in the mirror of the West. For that reason, it is a source of great happiness to me that this book is coming out in a bilingual format from a publisher with a large overseas market.

Looking back, I must say that, for me, reconstructing old *minka* has been less a business than pure pleasure. After my early realization that elements in traditional architecture built up by past generations must not be changed, I actually felt freer than ever. Once a job began, images would flood my mind, ideas springing up one after another. Sometimes I would wake up at night and turn them over sleeplessly, inducing my wife to comment, "You can't build houses in the middle of the night!" A visit to the site of a work-in-progress always inspired me with fresh ideas. I don't know how many times I changed my plan midway, even after the lumber was processed and work was coming along, knowing full well that I must pay all extra charges. I was blessed with builders who understood what I was after and worked unstintingly to produce superior architecture.

Whenever I asked the carpenters of Gujo to leave their families and go off with me to some faraway site, we never lacked for local miso and pickles. Women who provided the wherewithal for old-fashioned country meals were essential to the success of our endeavors. When no one else was available, I could always rely on my parents or my wife: we'd pack up cooking pans and rice pot, and live for a time like gypsies. Nowadays, wherever you go there are business hotels with capsule rooms to turn to, but I look back with infinite nostalgia on those early days. Those old cooking implements are like war buddies, and I can never throw them away.

Everything I may have done, I owe to the support of my wife, as well as to my parents, brother, and foster father, retired Associated Press Correspondent John Roderick. My beloved father died three years ago without living to see the publication of this book. I am also indebted to the carpenters of Gujo, Fumio Katagiri and Takao Sumi; and to Eishi Sanjo of Chiba and the many other craftsmen it has been my privilege to get to know.

Compared to architecture, publishing a book seemed a much more dubious adventure. Fortunately Akira Amakasu, a seasoned editor, was most helpful and led me every step of the way. I must also express sincere thanks to the photographers who took so many great shots; to Michiko Hiraoka of Kodansha International, who laid the initial groundwork for the book; and to Michiko Uchiyama, Kazuhiko Miki, and Barry Lancet, who graciously took over thereafter.

YOSHIHIRO TAKISHITA

あとがき

　ダムに沈むことになった和泉村の合掌造り民家を、鎌倉の山の上に移築して古民具や伊万里の店を開いたのは、30年前、私が26歳の時である。若さの気まぐれで開いたような店であったが、東京から程良い距離という地の利もあったのだろうか。各国の大使館や、外国の企業から日本にやってくるVIPを紹介されることが多く、王室、オペラ歌手、芸術家の方々など多彩な人々をお迎えすることができた。どの人も例外なく建物に関心を示し「ほんとうに気持ちの休まる空間だ」「いつまでもここに座っていたい」などといわれた。マンスフィールド駐日米国大使の "Here is Japan" の一言は心に残っている。カリフォルニア州に大邸宅を持つアメリカ人が来訪されたのは1984年であったが、たいへん気に入られ「私の邸宅と取り替えようではないか」とまでいわれ、若い私は有頂天にさせられた。

　移築の注文も最初は外国の方が多く、私の仕事は欧米という鏡に照らされながら進んできた。その意味からいっても、海外に市場をもつ出版社から和英両文を付けての出版となったことは喜ばしい限りである。

　振り返ってみると、民家移築の仕事は、私にとってはビジネスという以上に、純粋な楽しみですらあった。ごく初期の段階で、先人の積み重ねた伝統的な建築には、くずしてはならない部分があることを悟ってからは、かえって発想が自由になった。ひとつの仕事が始まると、次々とイメージが浮かび、アイディアが湧いてくる。夜中に目が醒めてあれこれ考え眠れない時、妻から「夜中に家は建てられませんよ」といわれたほどである。そして、現場へ行くと、また新しいアイディアが浮かぶ。材木の加工もすみ、工事も進んでいて、費用はこちらの持ち出しとなるのを承知で思い通りに変更したことが何度あっただろう。私の意をくんで良き建築のために力を惜しまない大工さんたちにも恵まれていた。

　郡上の大工さんたちに家族を離れて遠い建築現場へ行ってもらう時、郡上の味噌と漬け物は欠かせず、昔風の田舎料理のできる賄いの小母さんは大切な戦力であった。人手のないときはやむを得ず両親や妻をかりだし、鍋や釜を持って移動するジプシーのような生活だった。今ではビジネスホテルに個室という時代に変化したが、あの頃のなつかしい鍋や釜は戦友のようでとても捨てられない。

　私を支えてくれた妻、そして両親、兄たちのおかげで今まで無事やってこれたと思う。私が敬愛した父はこの本の出版を待たずに3年前他界した。郡上の大工さんの片桐文雄氏と鷲見隆男氏たち、千葉の三條さんをはじめたくさんの職人さんたちには感謝の念で一杯だ。

　建築に比べると、出版は心もとないかぎりであった。さいわい老練な出版人である甘糟章氏が施主のひとりであったので親しく相談に乗って頂くことができた。文字通り手取り足取りのご指導を受けた。数々の撮影にご協力くださったカメラマンの方々、出版の骨組みを作りスタートさせていただいた講談社インターナショナルの平岡美智子さん、その後を引き継いでくださった内山通子さん、バリー・ランセットさん、デザイン部の三木和彦さんにもあらためてお礼申し上げたい。

瀧下嘉弘

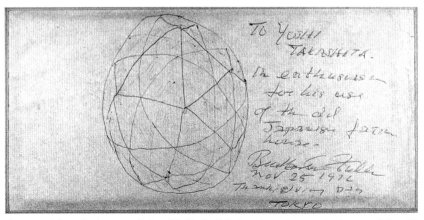

A postcard from Buckminster Fuller: "To Yoshi Takishita, In enthusiasm for his use of the old Japanese farm house."

世界的に著名な建築家バックミンスター・フラー氏から頂いた励ましの言葉。

PUBLISHER'S ACKNOWLEDGMENT

The publisher would like to gratefully acknowledge Philip Harper and Juliet Winters Carpenter for their fine translations; Azby Brown for his assistance with the architectural aspects of the text and for so ably conveying the author's ideas into English for the captions; Tadamistu Omori for his excellent line drawings and tracings of the floor plans; Ayako Adachi for her translation of the Foreword into Japanese; and Ralph Cassel and Judith Ravin for assistance in copyediting and proofreading.

協力

翻訳：フィリップ・ハーパー、ジュリエット・ウィンターズ・カーペンター、足立恵子
編集協力：アズビー・ブラウン
図版：大森忠光
校正：ラルフ・カッスル、ジュディス・ラビン、株式会社プレス

PHOTO CREDITS

Keishi Asaoka 浅岡敬史 pages 70-71, 72 (top, bottom right), 73 (top).

Hashet Fujin Gaho-sha アシェット婦人画報社 The photographs by Tadahiro Kumagai were originally published in *Modern Living* magazine and appear here courtesy of Hashet Fujin Gaho-sha. Noboru Murata's photograph on pages 42-43 (center) first appeared in *Elle Deco* magazine, also published by Hashet Fujin Gaho-sha.
熊谷忠宏氏撮影の写真は「モダンリビング」編集部のご厚意により掲載、また村田昇氏撮影の42-43ページ（中央）の写真は「エル・デコ」編集部のご厚意により掲載させて頂きました。

Ryo Hata 畑亮 pages 1-7, 11, 27-29, 35 (bottom), 40, 45-46, 51, 59, 134-35, 137, 139-41, 151.

Isao Hirachi 平地勲 pages 74-77, 79.

Toru Iijima 飯島徹 pages 10, 22-23, 32-33, 34-35 (bottom), 35 (top), 36-39, 42 (left), 43 (right), 44, 47-50, 52-53, 55, 58 (top), 61-69, 72 (bottom left), 73 (bottom), 78 (right), 82, 84, 91 (top and bottom), 97 (bottom left), 98-125, 136, 138, 153-54, 155 (top left), 156 (top), 157.

Tadahiro Kumagai 熊谷忠宏 pages 40-41 (center), 78 (left), 81, 83, 85-90, 92-96, 97 (top, bottom right).

Noboru Murata 村田昇 pages 30-31, 34 (top left, bottom left), 35 (right center), 42-43 (center), 56-57, 58 (bottom), 126-33, 142-50, 152, 155 (top left, bottom left, bottom right), 158 (all).

Kiyoshi Takai 高井潔 pages 14-15, 19.

Yoshimi Wakui 和久井義三 page 156 (bottom left, bottom right).

みんかいちく
民家移築
Japanese Country Style

2002 年 4 月26日　第 1 刷発行

著　者　瀧下嘉弘
発行者　野間佐和子
発行所　講談社インターナショナル株式会社
　　　　〒112-8652 東京都文京区音羽 1-17-14
　　　　電話　03-3944-6493（編集部）
　　　　　　　03-3944-6492（営業部・業務部）
　　　　ホームページ　http://www.kodansha-intl.co.jp
印刷所　大日本印刷株式会社
製本所　牧製本印刷株式会社

落丁本・乱丁本は、小社業務部宛にお送りください。送料小社負担にてお取替えします。なお、この本についてのお問い合わせは、編集部宛にお願いいたします。本書の無断複写（コピー）、転載は著作権法の例外を除き、禁じられています。

定価はカバーに表示してあります。

Copyright © 2002 by Yoshihiro Takishita
Printed in Japan
ISBN 4-7700-2761-3